TUSCANY

TUSCANY
AN ANTHOLOGY

Compiled by Laura Raison
Foreword by John Julius Norwich

Ebury Press
London

For Grandpa and Marpy,
armchair travellers

Published by Ebury Press
Division of The National Magazine Company Ltd
Colquhoun House
27-37 Broadwick Street
London W1V 1FR

ISBN 0 85223 550 X
Cover photograph: Gerd von Bassewitz/Susan Griggs Agency
Printed in Great Britain at the University Press, Cambridge

CONTENTS

FOREWORD

BY JOHN JULIUS NORWICH

For most of us, Tuscany is the quintessence of Italy, the distillation of all those elements of the country that we think of as being most specifically Italian. Rome is overlaid by antiquity and Catholicism; Milan, one feels, has sold out to industry and international big business; Venice remains what she has always been – *sui generis,* a law unto herself. But Florence and Siena, Pisa and Arezzo and all the smiling countryside around them, with its hill-top villages, its olive groves and its cypresses straight out of a background by Simone Martini or Benozzo Gozzoli – they, surely, are Italian through and through. Even the Italian language as we know it today is in reality the Tuscan dialect, adopted – often unwillingly – by the rest of the peninsula only because it was the medium of the first, and still the greatest, masterpiece of Italian literature, the *Divine Comedy.* And so perfect an instrument has it proved to be that in nearly seven centuries it has hardly changed. Relatively few of us can today enjoy *The Canterbury Tales* in the original without a crib or at least a dictionary, and the French have much the same trouble with the *Roman de la Rose;* but for anyone with a working knowledge of modern Italian, the language of Dante – who lived, be it remembered, well before Chaucer and was a contemporary of Jean de Meung – need have no terrors.

Laura Raison knows Tuscany and loves it; and both her knowledge and her love are revealed in this anthology. So, indeed, is her industry. In compiling this glorious celebration of all things Tuscan she has ranged widely and dug deep; and her task can have been made no easier by the sheer quantity of material, in the English language alone, through which she has had to sift. From the early nineteenth century onwards, English travellers flocked to Tuscany; and a large proportion of them wrote copiously of what they saw and felt. The vogue was started, it need hardly be said, by John Ruskin – Sir Kenneth Clark used to attribute the overwhelming preference of Victorian travellers for Florence over Venice to the fact that *The Stones of Venice* consisted of three immense and largely unreadable volumes, whereas *Mornings in Florence* was a slim and unpretentious work which slipped comfortably into the pocket of one's Norfolk jacket. Then, as the century progressed, a new element made its appearance: the murmur of well-bred county voices in the English tea-rooms beside the Arno was increasingly intermingled with the accents of New York and Boston, and was occasionally hushed altogether, into reverential silence, by the rotund ponderosities of Henry James.

The Brownings and Hawthorne, Berenson, Forster and Pound – so the list goes on; and all this is to say nothing of the Italians who, very properly, fill many of these pages, a number of them being giants of the Renaissance in their own right – Michelangelo, Machiavelli, Lorenzo the Magnificent and Galileo, to name only the first that come to mind. Then there are Frenchmen like Stendhal, Germans like Heine, Russians like Anna Akhmatova and Alexander Blok; even Pliny the Younger is allowed to have his say. There must, I suspect, have been times when Miss Raison felt close to despair at the magnitude of her task. But she has accomplished it, triumphantly, and in doing so she has brought back to us the old Tuscany, the Tuscany whose foreign visitors were travellers rather than tourists, who knew what they wanted to see and understood it when they saw it. For this reason, the pleasure that we gain from her anthology may at moments be tinged with sadness for a world, and a whole way of life, that has gone. But it remains a pleasure still – for which, as for the countless, previously unfamiliar treasures, which she has unearthed, transcribed and where necessary translated for our enjoyment, all lovers of Italy have good cause to be grateful.

John Julius Norwich (1983)

INTRODUCTION

For my grandparents' generation it was Berenson and the Sitwells, for my parents' it was the Pieros at Borgo San Sepolcro, but for me it was a melon and raspberry ice-cream outside Vivoli's in Florence that first convinced me that Tuscany was the place to be. We came and went, like many summer visitors, squashed into a car like a furnace and staying in cool, dark villas or pensions with tiled floors and roadworks outside. Other visitors have come to Tuscany in coaches, on horseback and on foot, and when the Arno valley was still marshland Hannibal in the third century B.C. arrived on an elephant.

Today's travellers are usually less warlike as they wander from town to town, eating and taking photographs, displaying their nationalities as clearly as if they were carrying their contrada banner in the Palio. The English in particular have the peculiar habit of comparing everything with England. Norman Douglas saw Viareggio as 'a rowdy place in summer; not rowdy however after the fashion of Margate'. Leigh Hunt's Leghorn was a 'polite Wapping', and even Ruskin denounced the 'Newgate-like palaces' of Florence. The towns go in and out of fashion. But Siena is always 'in' and Viareggio increasingly 'out', except with the lounging boys who work for Fiat in Turin and the vast women in black bathing suits and straw hats.

Many travellers seduced, as you cannot fail to be, by the loveliness of the landscape and the beauty of man's creations, made Tuscany their home and settled permanently. So, an English colony took root, which like most expatriate communities remained thoroughly British. Its members absorbed the sunlight and did the things they liked best, adopting Italy in their minds as their own country, but not usually mixing much with the Tuscans.

'The Anglo-American visitors . . . as it were, expropriated Florence occupying villas at Fiesole or Bellosguardo, studying Tuscan wild-flowers, collecting ghost stories, collecting triptychs and diptychs, burying their dogs in the churchyard of the Protestant Episcopal church, knowing (for the most part) no Florentines but their servants.' (Mary McCarthy 1959).

In the country, among the remoter Tuscan hills, it is hard not to feel overwhelmed by the oldness – the feeling that everything has remained unchanged for hundreds or thousands of years. You can scramble up the terraces or over the southern hills, through vines, olives and cypresses, to where a few farmers still use the ancient white oxen for ploughing. There is a feeling of continuity. Galileo, Dante, or even Virgil, would not look out of place against this landscape. H.V. Morton expressed the experience of many visitors on coming across a farmer or Post-office worker, 'I looked up and found myself gazing at the taut lean face of Cosimo de Medici', for even the village men leaning casually against a café door seem to bear a strong resemblance to the portraits of their ancestors.

In the larger towns, and in particular, Florence, there is an aura of trade, of commerce, various industries and workshops. Only a few Italians seem interested in who comes and who goes, and they belong mainly to the tourist trade. In summer in Florence there is a noise problem, a traffic problem, a smell problem, and certainly a heat problem. Not everyone finds it a pleasant place. But in the older parts of the city on a summer night even the least historically minded can picture groups of young men in fifteenth century dress singing or brawling through the streets, perpetuating the interminable squabbles of the centuries before. It was with some cause that Dante accused the Florentines of making a gallows of their own home. Watching the growing numbers of buskers, jugglers and mime shows in the Piazza della Signoria it is easy to imagine that the faint smell of smoke is from the fire where Savonarola was burned as a heretic in 1498. The past invades Florence, all mixed up with the modern town – the buzzing Vespas, the railway station and postcard stands.

In Tuscany, perhaps more than any other place, history has been immortalized on canvas and in marble, and the artists and writers who brought fame to their land are accessible to even the most casual of visitors. On our first visit to Florence we made the classic mistake that so many people, pressed for time, must make, of 'doing' the whole Uffizi in one morning. We emerged finally, glutted and incredulous, depressed by the sheer amount of it all and the lack of time to explore it. Apart from the quality there is such a tremendous quantity of things to see that it is impossible to know where to start. There will never be enough time, except for the lucky ones with houses in the area – and perhaps not even for them. It is best to choose just a few things, and then to go as slowly as you like, through the dim cool churches and monasteries, the strange striped cathedrals and solid palaces, each more interesting and beautiful than the last. And when you have done enough for one day, stop, and wander round the narrow streets for a while, or sit down in a café and order some wine.

I have tried through the writings of inhabitants and guests, painters and politicians to evoke the spirit of the place, so that whether you are sitting under a cypress near Poppi or on a bench in Paddington Station Tuscany and all her splendour never need be far away.

L.R. (1983)

CHAPTER 1

BEGINNINGS

After Andrea del Sarto (1705-1885), Study for Head of Jesus
Victoria and Albert Museum Crown ©

I went to sleep at dawn in Tuscany
Beneath a rock and dreamt a morning dream.
I thought I stood by that baptismal stream
Whereon the bounds of our redemption lie.
And there, beyond, a radiance rose to take
My soul at passing, in which light your eyes
So filled me I was drunk with Paradise.
Then the day broadened, but I did not wake.

Here's the last edge of my long parchment furled,
And all was writ that you might read it so.
This sleep I swear shall last the length of day;
Not noise, not chance, shall drive this dream away:
Not time, not treachery, not good fortune - no,
Not all the weight of all the wears of the world.

Hilaire Belloc (1870-1953)

ETRUSCAN PLACES

The origin of the Etruscans is still a matter for dispute, although at the height of their power they spread from the Po down to Campania. It is widely felt that European culture owes a great deal to this ancient civilization.

. . . in those days, on a fine evening like this, the men would come in naked, darkly ruddy-coloured from the sun and wind, with strong, insouciant bodies; and the women would drift in, wearing the loose, becoming smock of white or blue linen; and somebody, surely, would be playing on the pipes; and somebody, surely, would be singing, because the Etruscans had a passion for music, and an inner carelessness the modern Italians have lost. The peasants would enter the clear, clean, sacred space inside the gates, and salute the gay-coloured little temple as they passed along the street that rose uphill towards the arx, between rows of low houses with gay-coloured fronts painted or hung with bright terra-cottas. One can almost hear them still, calling, shouting, piping, singing, driving in the mixed flocks of sheep and goats, that go so silently, and leading the slow, white, ghostlike oxen with the yokes still on their necks.

And surely, in those days, young nobles would come splashing in on horseback, riding with naked limbs on an almost naked horse, carrying probably a spear, and cantering ostentatiously through the throng of red-brown, full-limbed, smooth-skinned peasants. A Lucumo, even, sitting very noble in his chariot driven by an erect charioteer, might be driving in at sundown, halting before the temple to perform the brief ritual of entry into the city. And the crowding populace would wait; for the Lucumo of the old days, glowing ruddy in flesh, his beard stiffly trimmed in the Oriental style, the torque of gold round his neck, and the mantle or wrap bordered with scarlet falling in full folds, leaving the breast bare, he was divine, sitting on the chair in his chariot in the stillness of power. The people drew strength even from looking at him.

The chariot drew a little forward, from the temple; the Lucumo, sitting erect on his chair in the chariot, and bare-shouldered and bare-breasted, waits for the people. Then the peasants would shrink back in fear. But perhaps some citizen in a white tunic would life up his arms in salute, and come forward to state his difficulty, or to plead for justice. And the Lucumo, seated silent within another world of power, disciplined to his own responsibility of knowledge for the people, would listen till the end. Then a few words – and the chariot of gilt bronze swirls off up the hill to the house of the chief, the citizens drift on to their houses, the music sounds in the dark streets, torches flicker, the whole place is eating, feasting, and as far as possible having a gay time.

It is different now. The drab peasants, muffled in ugly clothing, straggle in across the waste bit of space, and trail home, songless and meaningless. We have lost the art of living; and in the most important science of all, the science of daily life, the science of behaviour, we are complete ignoramuses.

Brute force crushes many plants. Yet the plants rise again. The pyramids will not last a moment compared with the daisy. And before Buddha or Jesus spoke the nightingale sang, and long after the words of Jesus and Buddha are gone into oblivion the nightingale still will sing. Because it is neither preaching nor teaching nor commanding nor urging. It is just singing. And in the beginning was not a Word, but a chirrup.

Because a fool kills a nightingale with a stone, is he therefore greater than the nightingale? Because the Roman took the life out of the Etruscan, was he therefore greater than the Etruscan? Not he! Rome fell, and the Roman phenomenon with it. Italy to-day is far more

Etruscan in its pulse than Roman: and will always be so. The Etruscan element is like the grass of the field and the sprouting of corn, in Italy: it will always be so. Why try to revert to the Latin-Roman mechanism and suppression?

D.H.Lawrence (1885-1930)

Roadside Songs of Tuscany.

Many Tuscan folksongs were originally brought to light by Ruskin, but translated and illustrated by Francesca Alexander who described them to Ruskin thus:
  'These songs and hymns of the poor people have been collected, little by little, in the course of a great many years which I have passed in constant intercourse with the Tuscan Contadini. They are but the siftings, so to say, of the hundreds and hundreds which I have heard and learnt, mostly from old people: many of them have never, so far as I know, been written down before, and others it would be impossible now to find' (1859). However, other rhymes in the same mode have also emerged from other sources.

A REAPER

The first time that I saw you, maiden fair,
Was in a cornfield where you came and reaped:
You'd tucked your skirt up well, and then and there
You set to work, and quick the row you sweeped:
I saw you working, and your way admired;
I saw you fair, and that my love inspired.

Tuscan Folk Rhyme

ANNUNCIATION: LEONARDO (R.F.)

There was never a morning quite so tremendous again.
The birth, you think? I'm not for setting great store
By birth. Births aren't beginnings. And anyway
She only wanted to sleep off the pain
Which had made her a beast among beasts on the cowhouse floor.
Shepherds and magnates tiptoeing through the hay

Leonardo da Vinci (1452-1519), Above: Detail from The Annunciation
Uffizi Gallery (Photo Alinari). *Below: The Annunciation*

(You get all kinds at an inn, she drowsily thought),
Even the babe – they were part of a snowdrift trance,
Almost unreal. He was to prove a good son
In his way, though his way was beyond her. Whatever he sought
When he left home and led his friends such a dance,
He did not forget her as other boys might have done.

Her morning of mornings was when one flew to bring
Some news that changed her cottage into a queen's
Palace; the table she worked at shone like gold,
And in the orchard it is suddenly spring,
All bird and blossom and fresh-painted green.
What was it the grand visitor foretold
Which made earth heaven for a village Mary?
He was saying something about a Saviour Prince,
But she only heard him say, 'you will bear a child',
And that was why the spring came. Angels carry
Such tidings often enough, but never since
To one who in such blissful ignorance smiled.

Cecil Day Lewis (1904-1972)

PAOLO AND FRANCESCA

*The story of Paolo and Francesca has become one of the most famous parts of Dante's
'Inferno' and a popular Tuscan folk tale. It tells how the daughter of the count of
Ravenna fell in love with the brother of her ordained husband Giovanni Malatesta
of Rimini. When the couple's affair was discovered they were both put to death in
1289. In 'Inferno' Francesca tells Dante how their love started.*

But if you have such a desire to know
The first root of our love, then I will tell you,
Although to do so, it will be as if I wept.

One day, when we were reading, for distraction,
How Lancelot was overcome by love -
We were alone, without any suspicion;

Several times, what we were reading forced
Our eyes to meet, and then we changed colour;
But one page only was more than we could bear.

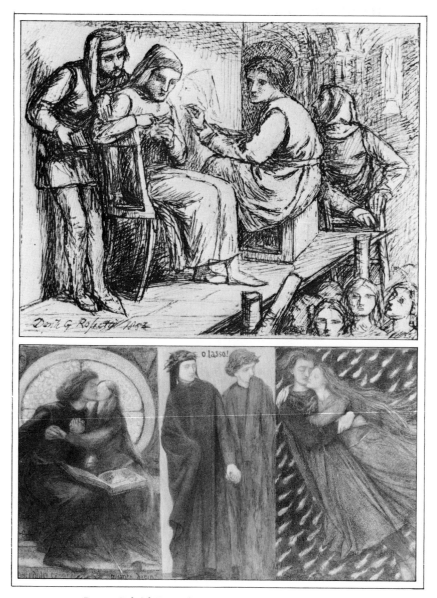

Dante Gabriel Rossetti (1828-1882) Tate Gallery London
Above: Study for 'Giotto painting Dante's Portrait', Below: Paolo and Francesca

When we read how that smile, so much desired,
Was kissed by such a lover, in the book,
He, who will never be divided from me,

Kissed my mouth, and the two of us were trembling.
The book, the writer played the part of Galahalt:
That day we got no further with our reading.

Dante Alighieri (1265-1321)
Translated by C.H. Sisson (1914-)

Quant' è bella giovinezza
Che si fugge tuttavia!
Chi vuol esser lieto, sia;
Di doman non c'è certezza.

How fair is youth, and how fast it flies away. Let him who will be merry,
of tomorrow nothing is certain.

Lorenzo de Medici (1449-92)

Sodoma (1477-1549), Detail from fresco Monte Oliveto Maggiore (Photo Alinari)

CHAPTER 2

FLORENCE

Take one bowl, one valley
Assisted by hills to peace
And let the hills hold back the wind a little
Only turning the trees
Only dividing the shadows
With a simple movement of sun
Across the valley's face.

And then set cypresses up,
So dark they seem to contain their repeated shadows
In a straight and upward leap,
So dark that the sun seems to avoid them to show
How austere they are, stiff admonishing gestures
Towards the city, yet also protective
To the deep houses that the sun makes more deep.

Here I say the mind is open, is freed.
Anchored only to frailest thoughts we are
Triumphantly subdued to the light's full glare.
It is simple then to be a stranger,
To have a mind that is wide
To permit the city to settle between our thoughts,
As between those hills, and flower and glow inside.

Elizabeth Jennings (1926-)

THE APPROACH TO FLORENCE

As we approached Florence, the country became cultivated to a very
high degree, the plain was filled with the most beautiful villas, and, as
far as the eye could reach, the mountains were covered with them; for
the plains are bounded on all sides by blue and misty mountains. The
vines are here trailed on low trellises of reeds interwoven into crosses
to support them, and the grapes, now almost ripe, are exceedingly
abundant. You everywhere meet those teams of beautiful white oxen,
which are now labouring the little vine-divided fields with the Virgilian
ploughs and carts. Florence itself, that is the Lung' Arno (for I have
seen no more), I think is the most beautiful city I have yet seen. It is

surrounded with cultivated hills and from the bridge which crosses the broad channel of the Arno, the view is the most animated and elegant I ever saw. You see three or four bridges, one apparently supported by Corinthian pillars, and the white sails of the boats, relieved by the deep green of the forest, which comes to the water's edge, and the sloping hills covered with bright villas on every side. Domes and steeples rise on all sides, and the cleanliness is remarkably great. On the other side there are the foldings of the Vale of Arno above; first the hills of olive and vine, then the chestnut woods, and then the blue and misty pine forest, which invest the aerial Apennines, that fade in the distance. I have seldom seen a city so lovely at first sight as Florence.

Percy Bysshe Shelley (1792-1822)

ON FIRST ARRIVING IN FLORENCE

The day before yesterday, as I descended upon Florence from the high ridges of the Apennine, my heart was leaping wildly within me. What utterly childish excitement! At long last, at a sudden bend in the road, my gaze plunged downward into the heart of the plain, and there, in the far distance, like some darkling mass, I could distinguish the sombre pile of *Santa Maria del Fiore* with its famous Dome, the masterpiece of Brunelleschi.

'Behold the home of Dante, of Michelangelo, of Leonardo da Vinci', I mused within my heart. 'Behold then this noble city, the Queen of mediaeval Europe! Here, within these walls, the civilisation of mankind was born anew; here it was that Lorenzo de Medici so brilliantly sustained the part of Kingship, and established a Court at which, for the first time since the reign of Augustus, military prowess was reduced to a secondary role. As the minutes passed, so these memories came crowding and jostling one against the other within my soul, and soon I found myself incapable of rational thought, but rather surrendered to the sweet turbulence of fancy, as in the presence of some beloved object. Upon approaching the San Gallo gate, with its unbeautiful Triumphal Arch, I could gladly have embraced the first inhabitants of Florence whom I encountered.

At the risk of losing all that multitude of personal belongings which a man accumulates about him on his travels, immediately the ceremony of the passport had, with fitting ritual, been observed, I abandoned my conveyance. So often have I studied views of Florence

14

that I was familiar with the city before I ever set foot within its walls; I found that I could thread my way through the streets without a guide. Turning to the left, I passed before a bookseller's shop, where I bought a couple of descriptive surveys of the town. Twice only was I forced to enquire my way of passers-by, who answered me with a politeness which was wholly French and with a most singular accent; and at last I found myself before the facade of Santa Croce.

Within, upon the right of the doorway, rises the tomb of Michelangelo; beyond, lo! there stands Canova's effigy of Alfieri; I needed no *cicerone* to recognise the features of the great Italian writer. Further still, I discovered the tomb of Machiavelli; while facing Michelangelo lies Galileo. What a race of men! And to these already named, Tuscany might further add Dante, Boccaccio and Petrarch. What a fantastic gathering! The tide of emotion which overwhelmed me flowed so deep that it scarce was to be distinguished from religious awe. My soul, affected by the very notion of being in Florence, and by the proximity of those great men, was already in a state of trance. Absorbed in the contemplation of sublime beauty, I could perceive its very essence close at hand; I could, as it were, feel the stuff of it beneath my fingertips. I had attained to that supreme degree of sensibility where the divine intimations of art merge with the impassioned sensuality of emotion. As I emerged from the port of Santa Croce, I was seized with a fierce palpitation of the heart; I walked in constant fear of falling to the ground.

Stendhal (1783-1842)

FLORENCE

Alexander Blok stayed in Florence for two months during the summer of 1909

I
Die, Florence, Judas, disappear
in the twilight of long ago!
In the hour of love and in the hour
of death I'll not remember you.

Oh, laugh at yourself today, Bella
for your features have fallen in.
Death's rotten wrinkles disfigure
that once miraculous skin.

15

The motorcars snort in your lanes,
your houses fill me with disgust;
you have given yourself to the stains
of Europe's bilious yellow dust.

The bicycles ring in the dust
where Savonarola faced the flame,
where Leonardo knew the dusk,
and where Beato's blue dream came.

Your sumptuous Medicis shudder,
your trampled lilies you deface,
but your own life you cannot recover
in the dust of the marketplace!

The slow groan of the Mass, the charnel
stink of roses in the nave -
may all that cumbersome ritual
melt in time's scouring wave!

II
You, Florence, are a tender iris.
For whom did I hunger and thirst
all day, with a love deep and hopeless,
in your Cascine gardens' dust?

How good to remember hopelessness,
to dream in your seclusion, stroll
in ancient heat and in the tenderness
of my no longer stripling soul . . .

But we are divorced by destiny,
and over far lands to the south
your smoky iris will return to me
in dreams like the days of my youth.

III
In a long and serene embrace
my soul is tightly bound,
the smoky iris, tender iris
breathing its fragrance round

Florence - The Duomo and Campanile   Monte Oliveto Maggiore (Photo Alinari)

commands me to cross rivers
on wings as the wind flies,
commands me to drown forever
deep in those twilit skies,
and when I surrender myself
to the last heat of the day,
blue heat, a blue wave in a gulf
of blue, will carry me away . . .

IV

Sunbeaten, burning stone scorches
my fever-misted sight.
Under the flame smoky irises
seem poised as if for flight.

O, inconsolable misery!
I know you by heart, despair!
Into the black sky of Italy
with a black soul I stare.

V

False windows on a black sky opening,
and a spotlight picking out a palace.
There she goes, in her patterned clothing
with a smile on her swarthy face.

And wine already troubles my sight
and its fire has entered my bloodstream . .
Signora, what shall I sing you tonight,
what shall I sing to sweeten your dream?

VI

Beneath the listless heat of Florence
your heart is emptier; carpeted
in silence are the steps of the churches;
and every flower hangs its head.

Keep a watch on the dregs of your heart
and have the artist's lie in mind:
for only in the skiff of art
can you leave the dreary world behind.

VII

In a blue smoke haze
rises the evening heat,
ruler of Tuscany . . .

On and on it sways
under lamps in the street
like a bat in no hurry . . .

Already in the valleys
lights without number glow,
and from the jeweller's window
gleam answering galaxies,
and mountains have eclipsed
the town with blue twilight;
with street songs on their lips
signore welcome the night.

The iris smokes in the dust,
in the Lacryma Christi
a light foam rises . . .

Dance and sing at the feast,
Florence, you deceiver,
in a wreath of scorched roses . . .

Incite my blood to madness
with passionate songs,
and make the night sleepless
and break the strings
and beat your tambourine,
to drown the sobs that rise
out of an empty lane
where your soul cries . . .

Alexander Blok (1880-1921)
Translated by Stallworthy and France (1970)

19

The Sanfrediano quarter is on the wrong side of the Arno, a huge pile of houses that lies along the left bank of the river, between the church of the Carmine and the slopes of Bellosguardo. Seen from above, it seems to be surrounded by the Medicean bastions and Palazzo Pitti, as if they were buttresses; and there the Arno runs at its widest, finding gentle, broad, and wonderful the curve that washes the Cascine gardens. Whenever civilization has become nature itself, the smile of God, terrible, fascinating and immobile, what perfection remains then, surrounds Sanfrediano and exalts it. But all is not gold that glisters. By contrast, Sanfrediano is the unhealthiest section of the city; in the heart of its streets, as densely populated as anthills, are located the Central Refuse Dump, the public dormitory, the barracks. The greater part of its slums is the home of rag-pickers, and of those who cook the intestines of cattle to make their living from them and from the broth that is the product. The broth, by the way, is tasty, and the Sanfredianini, who despise it, are nourished on it and buy it by the gallon.

The houses are ancient because of their stones, and even more because of their squalor. One backed up against another, they form an immense block, broken here and there by the openings of the side streets, where the sudden, incredible breezes enter from the river, and by the squares, vast and airy, extended harmoniously, like parade grounds. The happy, bickering clamour of the people brings these places to life: the sounds of the second-hand man and the rag-picker, the worker in the nearby repair shops, the office clerk, the artisan who works with gold, or in marble, or with furs. And even the women, most of them, have a job. Sanfrediano is a little republic of women who do work at home: they make the straw coverings that go around demijohns, they sew trousers, take in laundry, weave mats. With their work, subtracted from the cares of the house, they earn what they call the 'minimum extra' a family needs, when it is numerous - as they almost always are - and when the work of the man, if there is one, brings in only the bread and what goes with it.

The people of Sanfrediano, the toughest and liveliest of the Florentines, are the only ones who retain authentically the spirit of a people that has always been able to make something graceful even out of clumsiness, and whose ingenuity is a perpetual effrontery. The Sanfredianini are sentimental and pitiless at once: their idea of justice is symbolized by the enemy's remains hung to a lamp-post; and their idea of Paradise, summed up in a proverb, is poetic and vulgar: a Utopian place where there is an abundance of millet and a shortage of birds. They believe in God because, as they say, they believe 'in the hands and the eyes that made us'; and logically enough, reality seems to them finally the best of all possible dreams. Their hope lies in what they can make from day to day - which is never enough. Precisely because the foundation of their spirit is paved with incredulity, they are obstinate and active; and their participation in historic events has been intelligent, constant, even prophetic at times, though perhaps disordered. They have only covered over with more modern ideals their myths and banners; their light-heartedness, their intransigence, and their prejudices have remained the same. And if the shades of the Great move between Piazza della Signoria and the tombs of Santa Croce to light up the icy spirits of modernity with the sacred fire, then in the alley-ways of Sanfrediano the people that was contemporaneous with those Fathers moves still in flesh and blood, next door. The few of them who won a humble, malignant glory continue to exist; Boccaccio's Buffalmacco and Burchiello are alive. Those same women and maidens of whom the ancient romans and chronicles are full: lovely, genteel, audacious, shameless; those faces, the speech, the gestures in which chastity itself acquires a mysterious and irresistible enticement, and licentiousness becomes explicit, unaware and disarmed by candor - take one step here, and you meet them all.

Vasco Pratolini (1913-)
Translated by William Fense Weaver (1951)

We went to the Chuch of Santa Croce, from time to time, to weep over the tombs of Michael Angelo, Raphael and Machiavelli, (I suppose they are buried there, but it may be they reside elsewhere and rent their tombs to other parties - such being the fashion in Italy,) and between times we used to go and stand on the bridges and admire the Arno. It is popular to admire the Arno. It is a great historical creek with four feet in the channel and some scows floating around. It would be a very plausible river if they would pump some water into it. They all call it a river, and they honestly think it is a river, do these dark and bloody Florentines. They even help out the delusion by building bridges over it. I do not see why they are too good to wade.

Mark Twain (1835-1910)

I do not know what they are catching,
I only know that they stand there, leaning
A little like lovers, eager but not demanding,
Waiting and hoping for a catch, money,
A meal tomorrow but today, still there, steady.

And the river also moves as calmly
From the waterfall slipping to a place
A mind could match its thought with.
And above, the cypresses with cool gestures
Command the city, give it formality.

It is like this every day but more especially
On Sundays; every few yards you see a fisherman,
Each independent, none
Working with others and yet accepting
Others. From this one might, I think,

Build a whole way of living - men in their mazes
Of secret desires yet keeping a sense
Of order outwardly, hoping
Not too flamboyantly, satisfied with little
Yet not surprised should the river suddenly
Yield a hundredfold, every hunger appeased.

Elizabeth Jennings (1926-)

15 December 1895

Viale dei Colli, San Miniato in the most radiant weather. A sky now but softly overcast, now almost azure, which deepens toward evening because of the abundant mists: the whole city melts in a golden bake-oven. The roofs are plum-coloured; the Duomo with its campanile, the tower of the Palazzo Vecchio rise above the rest; the hills seem remote; the high mountain opposite Fiesole stands out. The wonderful Arno appears in places, as it enters and leaves the city. The sun is setting, bathing with soft and veiled glory this whole scene that we can see from the marble terraces of the cemetery, framed in by mortuary cypresses, almost black, severe and most appropriate to Florence.

Portrait of Unknown Youth by F. Salviati (1510-1563)

16th December 1895

Beautiful hills along the Arno from San Miniato to those opposite the Cascine. I am becoming more and more familiar with their contours of stern softness and their hues of green and grey.

Already the Arno has gone down considerably and this morning the mud-sifters reappeared - marsh workers who fill their flat boats with shovelfuls of silt dug up from the bottom or low shores of the river.

The day before yesterday, toward the end of the night, a violent storm burst out. Squall, hail, dumbfounding flashes of lightning and deafening thunder - nothing was missing - not even the full peal of the pre-Christmas bells which ring out toward dawn, desperately bewildered in the vast transport of the tempest, yet whose sound seems angelic in the early morning.

I expected on awakening to find a sky of washed azure; I see clouds and more clouds - a dramatic sky of deluge.

André Gide (1869-1951)
Translated by D. Bussey (1949)

RAIN IN FLORENCE

I am waiting for it to continue. I like it. From my chair by the door, peering through the cool silver strings, I can see that the entrance halls of these old palaces - vaulted shadowy vestibules, beautifully proportioned and with elegant leaping staircases of ancient iron or brass - have become more mysterious and suggestive than ever. What a strange disturbing quality they have! There is nearly always a lurking figure in the semi-dark, sometimes of a woman whose face or pose has a certain beauty; or of a draped stone statue supporting an incongruous bicycle - and one is scarcely sure, on passing, if the woman was a statue or the statue a woman - she could almost have been half and half. Or there is a wide-eyed youth, with an upturned bell that he does not ring. Or a little girl, barefooted, with a small bird on her head. There is something surrealist, sometimes at night faintly sinister, always provocative, in these short glimpses of entrance-halls in Florence. It seems to me that they are never quite empty, or that I have peopled them with half-remembered dreams...

Anthony Thorne (pub. 1957)

On the north side of the Arno, between Ponte Vecchio and Ponte Santa Trinità, is a row of immemorial houses that back on the river, in whose yellow flood they bathe their sore old feet. Anything more battered and befouled, more cracked and disjointed, dirtier, drearier, poorer, it would be impossible to conceive. They look as if fifty years ago the liquid mud had risen over their chimneys and then subsided again and left them coated forever with its unsightly slime. And yet forsooth, because the river is yellow, and the light is yellow, and here and there, elsewhere, some hint of colour, some accident of atmosphere, takes up the foolish tale and repeats the note - because, in short, it is Florence, it is Italy, and the fond appraiser, the infatuated alien, may have had in his eyes, at birth and afterwards, the micaceous sparkle of brown-stone fronts no more interesting than so much sand-paper, these miserable dwellings, instead of suggesting mental invocations to an enterprising board of health, simply create their own standard of felicity and shamelessly live in it. Lately, during the misty autumn nights, the moon has shone on them faintly and refined their shabbiness away into something ineffably strange and spectral. The turbid stream sweeps along without a sound, and the pale tenements hang above it like a vague miasmatic exhalation. The dimmest back-scene at the opera when the tenor is singing his sweetest, seems hardly to belong to a world more detached from responsibility.

Henry James (1843-1916)

WAKING

It was pleasant to wake up in Florence, to open the eyes upon a bright bare room, with a floor of red tiles which look clean though they are not; with a painted ceiling whereon pink griffins and blue amorini sport in a forest of yellow violins and bassoons. It was pleasant, too, to fling wide the windows, pinching the fingers in unfamiliar fastenings, to lean out into sunshine with beautiful hills, and trees and marble churches opposite, and, close below, the Arno, gurgling against the embankment of the road.

Over the river men were at work with spades and sieves on the sandy foreshore, and on the river was a boat, also diligently employed for some mysterious end. An electric tram came rushing underneath the window. No one was inside it, except one tourist; but its platforms were overflowing with Italians, who preferred to stand. Children tried to hang on behind, and the conductor, with no malice, spat in their faces to make them let go. Then soldiers appeared - good-looking, under-sized men - wearing each a knapsack covered with mangy fur, and a greatcoat which had been cut for some larger soldier. Beside them walked officers, looking foolish and fierce, and before them went little boys, turning somersaults in time with the band. The tram-car became entangled in their ranks, and moved on painfully, like a caterpillar in a swarm of ants. One of the little boys fell down, and some white bullocks came out of an archway. Indeed, if it had not been for the good advice of an old man who was selling buttonhooks, the road might never have got clear.

Over such trivialities as these many a valuable hour may slip away, and the traveller who has gone to Italy to study the tactile values of Giotto, or the corruption of the Papacy, may return remembering nothing but the blue sky and the men and women who live under it.

E.M. Forster (1879-1970)

AFTERNOON IN FLORENCE

This afternoon disturbs within the mind
No other afternoon, is out of time
Yet lies within a definite sun to end
In night that is in time. Yet hold it here
Our eyes, our minds, to make the city clear.

Light details no prisoner here at all
In brick or stone but sends a freedom out
Extends a shadow like a deeper thought,
Makes churches move, once still,
Rocking in light as music rocks the bell.

So eyes make room for light and
                minds make room
For image of the city tangible.
We look down on the city and a dream
Opens to wakefulness, and waking on
This peace perpetuates this afternoon.

Elizabeth Jennings (1926-)

A View of the common Fishing-Place without St. Fredians Gate at FLORENCE.

A VIEW of the Church and Piazza of All Saints at FLORENCE.

Traditionally on Holy Thursday after a service in the Duomo a man-made dove has been flown in the city - her flight symbolising prosperity and good luck.

Mass was now said at the high altar, but everyone's attention seemed to be concentrated on an unsightly high white post close to the marble balustrade which surrounds the altar. To this post was fixed a cord, which, suspended in mid-air far above the heads of the people, disappeared out of the great front door, and was fastened to the chariot outside the Duomo. A small white speck was seen on the cord, fastened to the pillar, which we were informed was the famous dove. When the *Gloria* had been sung, a man went up a ladder with a lighted taper, which he applied to the dove. There was a great spitting and hissing, and all at once she shot forward down the cord, a streak of fire and sparks. There was a stir and hum in the crowd, and a few little screams from some of the women; the dove vanished out of the door, and then there was a series of explosions from outside, while the dove returned as fast as she had gone, and went back to the pillar of wood, where she remained still fizzing for a few seconds.

Then all the bells of Florence, which had been silent since twelve o'clock on Thursday, began to ring merry chimes, and the great organ pealed out a triumphal melody. We made our way out of the Duomo as fast as we could, and were in time to see the last of the fire-works on the chariot; they made a tremendous noise, but as the sun shone brightly, there was not much to see. The fireworks were piled up some twenty feet high, and arranged in such a manner that only half of them go off in front of the Duomo, the other half being reserved for the corner of Borgo degli Albizzi, where the house of the Pazzi family is situated, in whose honour this custom was originally instituted. When all the squibs and crackers were finished, four magnificent white oxen, gaily decked with ribbons, were harnessed to the car, which moved off slowly with many creaks and groans round the south side of the cathedral towards the Via del Proconsolo. The crowd was immense, so we took some short cuts down the tortuous narrow streets in this old part of Florence, each of which has some passionate love-story or some dark tale of blood attached to it, and took up a favourable position opposite the entrance to the street of Borgo degli Albizzi, which is too narrow to admit the car.

The four white oxen were unharnessed and taken away, and a cord being put from the door of the Pazzi Palace to the car, another dove again flew to the fire-works, and the popping and fizzing was renewed, to the intense delight of the crowd.

The dove had flown swiftly and well this year, so the *contadini* returned home joyfully, spreading the glad tidings as they went - '*La colonada è andato bene*' (The dove has flown well).

Janet Ross (1842-1927)

DANTE'S FLORENCE

At first we cannot trace the Florence Dante knew. Nothing is less like the thirteenth-century Tuscan than the Tuscan of today; the powerful character, the wild and deep passion have given place to peaceable habits and gentle manners. A life of adventure, peril, and hate has been followed by pleasant indolence; we find nothing here of the concentrated violence of the Roman nature. Even the peasants of the neighbourhood of Florence have a certain elegance and sweetness of speech and address. The old mediaeval Tuscan type was gradually effaced by the hand of the Medici; the care of Leopold has succeeded in softening its lasting qualities.

Thus too is it with the aspect of Florence. At our first glance it seems quite modern. The main buildings themselves - the old strongholds which, like the Strozzi palace, make the streets dark beneath their dark and crenellated masses - are of a more recent date than that of Dante. The cathedral was scarcely begun in his time; and it took 166 years' work and the crowning gift of Brunelleschi to complete it. The only monument actually existing in Dante's time was the handsome Baptistery he loved so well and mentions as

'Il mio bel San Giovanni.'

Nevertheless, here and there, a few names or relics bring to mind Florence in the fourteenth century. By a fortunate chance there stood opposite to my window a wall with the funeral scutcheon of Charles of Valois - the *fleur de lis,* which for Dante was the symbol of proscription and exile, and which now is itself exiled and proscribed. If we look carefully, little by little we find the older Florence in the heart of the newer town. We may see a modern building grow above an ancient sub-structure: and French windows with green blinds above a wall of enormous black stones hewn diamond-wise. Here then are two epochs, one above another, just as on the Appian way the hovels of the rustics rise above the tombs of the ancient Romans.

29

The names of the streets take us back to Dante; often enough they belong to the persons or the families who are part of his poem. We find the street of the Blacks, the crucifix of the Whites, the street of the Ghibellines or of the Guelfs. As we cross these streets with their historic names, we can fancy that we shall run up against Farinata, Cavalcanti, or even Alighieri himself. The part of Florence where Dantesque recollections are centred is in the neighbourhood of the Cathedral and the Baptistery. Among the numerous square towers which here and there rise above the Florentine houses, there is one called the Tower of Dante. The stone of Dante, *sasso di Dante,* is not now to be found, but an inscription cut on a marble slab keeps alive the memory of this memory - the tradition of a tradition.

Finally, not far from here stands even to-day the Portinari palace, where there dwelt once a little girl who received the childish name of Bice. The youthful Dante, a lad of the neighbourhood, used to play with the child of the Portinari house, and for him thenceforward began the *new life* which he has so eloquently told; and there, in the soul of nine years' age, was sown the seed which was in later days to produce the immense poem devoted to the immortalisation of Beatrice.

Jean Jacques Ampère (d. 1864)

CHAPTER 3

TUSCAN TOWNS

Truly, one might as well try to describe the face of one's angel as these holy places of Pisa, which are catalogued in every guide-book ever written. At least I will withhold my hand from desecrating further that which is still so lovely. Only, if you would hear the heavenly choirs before death has his triumph over you, go by night into the Baptistery, having bribed some choir-boy to sing for you, and you shall hear from that marvellous roof a thousand angels singing round the feet of San Raniero.

Edward Hutton (1875-1969)

Friday, May 12th

Yes, Shelley chose better than Max Beerbohm. He chose a harbour; a bay; and his home, with a balcony, in which Mary stood, looks out across the sea. Sloping sailed boats were coming in this morning - a windy little town, of high pink and yellow southern homes, not much changed I suppose: very full of the breaking of waves, very much open to the sea; and the rather desolate house standing with the sea just in front. Shelley, I suppose, bathed, walked, sat on the beach there; and Mary and Mrs. Williams had their coffee on the balcony. I daresay the clothes and the people were much the same. At any rate, a very good great man's house in its way. What is the word for full of the sea? Can't think tonight, sky high in a bed-room at the Nettano in Pisa, much occupied by French tourists. The Arno swimming past with the usual coffee coloured foam. Walked in the cloisters: this is true Italy,with the old dusty smell; people swarming in the streets; under the - what is the word for - I think the word for a street that has pillars is Arcade. Shelley's house waiting by the sea, and Shelley not coming, and Mary and Mrs. Williams watching from the balcony and then Trelawney coming from Pisa and burning the body on the shore - that's in my mind. All the colours here are white bluish marble against a very light saturated sky. The tower leaning prodigiously. Clerical beggar at the door in a mock fantastic leather hat. The clergy walking. It was in these cloisters - Campo Santo - that L. and I walked 21 years ago and met the Palgraves and I tried to hide behind the pillars. And now we come in our car; and the Palgraves - are they dead, or very old? Now at any rate we have left the black country: the bald necked vulture country with its

The Leaning Bell-Tower, at Pisa

sprinkling of red-roofed villas. This is the Italy one used to visit in a railway train with Violet Dickinson - taking the hotel bus.

Virginia Woolf (1882-1941)

The appearance of Pisa gives me far more pleasure than that of Florence; the *lung' Arno* is so beautiful a sight, so wide and magnificent, so gay and smiling, that one falls in love with it. I have seen nothing like it in Florence, Milan, or Rome, and really I doubt whether in the whole of Europe many such sights could be found. It is a pleasure to stroll there in the winter, because the air is almost spring-like; and at certain hours of the day that part of the town is full of people, on foot or in carriages. One hears ten or twenty languages spoken, while brilliant sunshine lights up the gilding of the cafés, the shops full of frivolities, and the windows of the palaces and houses, all of fine architecture... As for the rest, Pisa is a blending of a big town and a little one, of town and country - a romantic combination, such as I have never seen elsewhere. To every other charm, its beautiful language must be added - and I will add, too, that I am well, am eating with appetite, and have a room looking out westwards over a great orchard - with so wide a view that one can see far towards the horizon.

Giacomo Leopardi (1798-1837) Translated by Iris Origo (1966)

EVENING: PONTE AL MARE, PISA

I

The sun is set; the swallows are asleep;
    The bats are flitting fast in the gray air;
The slow soft toads out of damp corners creep,
    And evening's breath, wandering here and there
Over the quivering surface of the stream,
Wakes not one ripple from its summer dream.

II

There is no dew on the dry grass to-night,
    Nor damp within the shadow of the trees;
The wind is intermitting, dry, and light;
    And in the inconstant motion of the breeze

The dust and straws are driven up and down,
And whirled about the pavement of the town.

III
Within the surface of the fleeting river
  The wrinkled image of the city lay,
Immovably unquiet, and forever
  It trembles, but it never fades away;
Go to the . . .
You, being changed, will find it then as now.

IV
The chasm in which the sun has sunk is shut
  By darkest barriers of cinereous cloud,
Like mountain over mountain huddled - but
  Growing and moving upwards in a crowd,
And over it a space of watery blue,
Which the keen evening star is shining through.

Percy Bysshe Shelley (1792-1822)

In the hour of evening, under a wintry sky amid whose darkly massed vapours a young moon is peering down upon this maddened world, I wander alone through deserted roadways towards that old solitary brick-tower. Here I stand and watch the Arno rolling its sullen waves. In Pisa, at such an hour, the Arno is the emblem of Despair. Swollen with melted snow from the mountains, it has gnawed its miserable clay banks and now creeps along, leaden and inert, half solid, like a torrent of liquid mud - irresolute whether to be earth or water; whether to stagnate here for ever at my feet, or crawl onward yet another sluggish league into the sea. So may Lethe look or Styx: the nightmare of a flood.

Norman Douglas (1868-1952)

CARRARA

It was a Sunday evening when I came to Carrara; all the world of labouring men and women was in the streets; in the piazza a band played; close to the hotel, in a tent set up for the occasion, a particularly atrocious collection of brass instruments were being blown with might

36

and main, to attract the populace to a marionette performance. The whole world seemed dizzy with noise. After dinner I went out into the streets among the people, but it was not any joy I found there, only a mere brutal cessation from toil in which, amid noise and confusion, the labourer sought to forget his labour. More and more as I went among them it seemed to me that the mountains had brutalised those who won from them their snowy treasure. In all Carrara and the valley of Torano I saw no beautiful or distinguished faces, - the women were without sweetness, the men a mere gang of workmen. Now common as this is in any manufacturing city of the North, it is very uncommon in Italy, where humanity has not been injured and enslaved by machinery as it has with us. You may generally find beauty, sweetness, or wisdom in the faces of a Tuscan crowd in any place. Only here you will see the man who has become just the fellow-labourer of the ox.

I understood this better when, about four o'clock on the next morning, I went in the company of a lame youth into the quarries themselves. There are some half-dozen of them, glens of marble that lead you into the heart of the mountains, valleys without shade, full of a brutal coldness, an intolerable heat, a dazzling light, a darkness that may be felt. Torano, that little town you came upon at the very threshold of the quarries, is like a town of the Middle Age, full of stones and refuse and narrow ways that end in a blind nothingness, and low houses without glass in the windows, and dogs and cats and animals of all sorts, goats and chickens and pigs, among which the people live. Thus busy with the frightful labour among the stones in the heart of the mountains, where no green thing has ever grown or even a bird built her nest, where in summer the sun looks down like some enormous moloch, and, in winter the frost and the cold scourge them to their labour in the horrid ghostly twilight, the people work. The roads are mere tracks among the blocks and hills of broken marble, yellow, black, and white stones, that are hauled on enormous trolleys by a line of bullocks in which you may often find a horse or a pony. Staggering along this way of torture, sweating, groaning, rebelling, under the whips and curses and kicks of the labourers, who either sit cursing on the wagon among the marble, or, armed with great whips, slash and cut at the poor capering, patient brutes, the oxen drag these immense wagons over the sharp boulders and dazzling rocks, grinding them in pieces, cutting themselves with sharp stones, pulling as though to break their hearts under the tyranny of the stones, not less helpless and insensate than they. At last, in a sort of despair, overwhelmed with heat and noise, you reach your inn, and though it be midday in July, you

seize your small baggage and set out where the difficult road leads out
of this spoiled valley to the olives and the sea.

Edward Hutton (1875-1969)

It was not till night that I reached the City of Lucca. How differently it
appeared to me the week before as I wandered by day through the
echoing deserted streets, and imagined myself transported to one of
those enchanted cities of which my nurse had so often told me. *Then* the
whole city was silent as the grave; all was so pale and death-like; the
gleam of the sun played on the roofs like gold-leaf on the head of a
corpse; here and there from the windows of a mouldering house hung
ivy tendrils like dried green tears, everywhere glimmering dreary and
dismally petrifying truth. The town seemed but the ghost of a town, a
spectre of stone in broad daylight. I sought long and in vain for some
trace of a living being. I can only remember that before an old Palazzo
lay a beggar sleeping with outstretched open hand. I also remember
having seen above at the window of a blackened mouldering little
house, a monk, whose red neck and plump shining pate, protruded
right far from his brown gown, and near him a full-breasted stark-
naked girl was visible, while below in the half-open house-door I saw
entering, a little fellow in the black dress of an abbé, and who carried
with both hands a mightly, full-bellied wine-flask. At the same instant
there rang not far off a delicately ironic little bell, while in my memory
tittered the novels of Messer Boccaccio. But these chimes could not
entirely drive away the strange shudder which ran through my soul. It
held me the more ironly bound since the sun lit up so warmly and
brightly the uncanny buildings; and I marked well that ghosts are far
more terrible when they cast aside the black mantle of night to show
themselves in the clear light of day.

But what was my astonishment at the changed aspect of the city
when I, eight days later, revisited Lucca. 'What is that?' I cried, as
innumerable lights dazzled my eyes and a stream of human beings
whirled through the streets. Has an entire race risen spectre-like from
the grave to mock *life* with the maddest mummery?' The previously
melancholy houses were bright with lamps, variegated carpets hung
from every window, nearly hiding the crumbling grey walls, and above
them peered out lovely female faces, so fresh, so blooming, that I well

marked that it was Life herself celebrating her bridal feast and Death who had invited the Beauty of Life as a guest. Yes, there marched behind the procession with a full accompaniment of drums and fifes, several companies of troops, besides which there was on each side near the priests in their flowing robes, grenadiers going by two and two. There were almost as many soldiers as clergy, but it requires many bayonets now-a-days to keep up religion and even when the blessing is given cannon must roar significantly in the distance.

Heinrich Heine (1797-1856) Translated by C. Leyland (1866)

Hitherto, all architecture, except fairy-finished Milan, had depended with me for its delight on being partly in decay . . . .

Here in Lucca I found myself suddenly in the presence of twelfth century buildings, originally set in such balance of masonry that they could all stand without mortar; and in material so incorruptible, that after six hundred years of sunshine and rain, a lancet could not now be put between their joints.

Absolutely for the first time I now saw what mediaeval builders were and what they meant. I took the simplest of facades for analysis, that of Santa Maria Foris-Portam, and thereon literally *began* the study of architecture.

John Ruskin (1819-1900)

Vasari in Arezzo

Arezzo is a small city and a charming one, simple, uncongested, comparatively quiet, and friendly, an enchanting backwater in the mainstream of tourism. My friend was proud of his famous fellow Aretines: Maecenas, the rich friend of Horace and Virgil, Petrarch, whose birthplace, now an Academy, was bombed during the last war, Guido of Arezzo, who devised musical notation, Leonardo Bruini, the historian of Florence, Pietro Aretino, the notorious journalist, feared and hated by so many, yet the bosom friend of Titian, and the artist-biographer, to whom all writers on art owe so much, Vasari, the author of *Lives of the Painters.* None of these, however, seems to have remained in his native town: Maecenas went to Rome, Petrarch to Avignon and Padua, Guido to Ferrara, Aretino to Venice; and the only one who established a home in Arezzo was Vasari, though it cannot have seen much of him.

His house exists much as it was in his time, and we walked up to the Via Venti Settembre to look at it. It is a fair-sized stone building of two storeys, and one enters it straight from the street to find oneself in the surroundings of a prosperous artist of the sixteenth century. How interesting it was, after having seen in Florence numbers of ducal walls decorated by Vasari and the suites of rooms designed by him in the Palazzo Vecchio, to stand in the simple surroundings which he designed for his own retirement. I was reminded of Giulio Romano's house in Mantua. It must have been pleasant for these artists and architects, after labouring for years on enormous rooms and lying on their backs painting ceilings, to come down to normal proportions and to rooms designed not to impress the beholder, but for ordinary living.

The chief room in Vasari's house has recessed windows and window-seats; there is a huge fireplace, and the walls and ceiling are richly decorated with the maze of classical allegory from which Vasari could apparently not extricate himself even in private life. However, even with a life-sized Venus over the mantlepiece, matched at the opposite side of the room by a many-breasted Diana of Ephesus, the room is a comfortable one in which a man could read and write and look out of the window to watch his friends passing in the street.

Unlike many artists, Vasari seems never to have been seriously short of money. He was a likeable, talented man with a tremendous capacity for work, and he must have been easier to get on with than geniuses who were temperamental and dilatory. Aged popes and cardinals, for whom time was a matter of some urgency, could feel confident, if they employed him, that the work would be done on time, and that was probably the foundation of his success. He was the son of a potter (which may explain the name Vasari), and he did not marry until he was well established and forty years of age. Having acquired his house when he was twenty-nine, the girls of Arezzo must long since have given him up as a confirmed bachelor. His eventual marriage, however, seems to have been a happy one, though childless.

How surprised he would have been could he have known that future ages would value his writings more than his paintings. His great classic was born one night at dinner when Cardinal Farnese suggested it would be a good idea to write the lives of Italian painters, sculptors, and architects. The year was 1544, when Vasari was thirty-three, and seven years later the first edition of his book was in print. All through his forties and fifties, while he was painting and building in Florence and Rome, he was gathering material for a second edition. The insatiable worker died in Florence at the age of sixty-three and was buried in Arezzo.

H.V. Morton (1892-1979)

The 'Giostra Del Saracino' *is a traditional Aretine custom.*

Every year on the first Sunday in September the Giostra del Saracino, the Joust of the Saracen, takes place in the Piazza. It is a revival of an old mediaeval game called the Quintana or Quintain, which afforded useful military training in the days when firearms had not been invented and knights could afford to be bold. For the joust the houses of the Piazza are beflagged - green and white on the north side, yellow and red on the east, green and red on the south and blue and yellow on the west, for the square is the traditional centre of the city where the four wards composing it all meet. Each owns a side, and the stands erected all round are decorated with the shield of their quarter. At the highest corner of the square, next to Vasari's Loggia, stands a wooden automaton in the form of a tall Saracen king. On his left arm hangs a shield divided into squares which are numbered one to five; his outstretched right arm holds a triple thong and at the end of it hang three leather globes the size of cricket balls. Beside him stand two live 'Saracens', whose duty is to untwist the cat-of-three-tails after use.

The four wards compete against each other and from early morning the streets are filled with processions of foot soldiers in mediaeval costume, each representing one of the four quarters. Knights on caparisoned horses in the colours of their ward are led along by grooms. Beautiful mediaeval ladies ride in the procession, their make-up by Elizabeth Arden and their costumes out of the Duc de Berry's *Book of Hours*. In the afternoon everyone assembles in the Piazza Grande. After parades by the costumed captains, standard-bearers, drummers, trumpeters and soldiers of the wards, eight knights, two for each ward, charge at full gallop up a gravelled runway which has been laid diagonally across the Piazza and lunge with their lances at the shield of the blackamoor. Each one tries to hit the square with the highest number. The Saracen rotates smartly on his axis when his shield is hit and if the knight is not very spry he is knocked off his horse by the cricket balls. Each knight is entitled to one charge but in the

41

event of a tie the leaders ride it off. Feeling runs high and the joust occasionally culminates in a free fight between the different wards.

A. Lyall (1904-1964)

AT SIENA

'Santa Caterina,/Fosti rosa senza spina/Giglio d'amore,/sposa del Signore'.

Hail Saint Catherine this morn,
Thou wast rose without a thorn,
Thou a lily wast of love,
Bride of our great Lord above.
Grant to me such favour kind
That at death I may not prove
One who lived in mortal sin!
May my spirit blessing win,
Blest in heaven and blest through life
Free us here from every strife!

Sienese Folk Rhyme

SIENA

Saturday, May 13th

Today we saw the most beautiful of views and the melancholy man. The view was like a line of poetry that makes itself; the shaped hill, all flushed with reds and greens; the elongated lines, cultivated every inch; old, wild, perfectly said, once and for all: and I walked up to a group and said 'What is that village? It called itself [l]'; and the woman with the blues eyes said, 'Won't you come to my house and drink?' She was famished for talk. Four or five of them buzzed round us and I made a Ciceronian speech about the beauty of the country. But I have no money to travel with, she said, wringing her hands. We would not go to her house - a cottage on the side of the hill: and shook hands: hers were dusty; she wanted to keep them from me; but we all shook hands and I wished we had gone to her house, in the loveliest of all landscapes. Then, lunching by the river, among the ants, we met the melancholy

42

man. He had five or six little fish in his hands, which he had caught in his hands. We said it was very beautiful country; and he said no, he preferred the town. He had been to Florence: no, he did not like the country. He wanted to travel, but had no money: worked at some village: no, he did not like the country, he repeated, with his gentle cultivated voice: no theatres, no pictures, only perfect beauty. I gave him 2 cigarettes; at first he refused, then offered us his six or seven little fish. We could not cook them at Siena, we said. No, he agreed, and so we parted.

It is all very well, saying one will write notes, but writing is a very difficult art. That is one has always to select: and I am too sleepy and hence merely run sand through my fingers. Writing is not in the least an easy art. Thinking what to write, it seems easy; but the thought evaporates, runs hither and thither. Here we are in the noise of Siena - the vast tunnelled arched stone town, swarmed over by chattering shrieking children.

[1] *left blank in her diary.*   *Virginia Woolf (1882-1941)*

SIENA CATHEDRAL

Siena Cathedral has the look of a bishop who, by some strange accident of highway robbery or shipwreck, has been obliged to assume an oriental costume. Nothing could be more Christian than the outlines of this noble church, and nothing more Moslem than the horizontal stripes of white and black marble with which it is built. As one looks at it, memories of other Gothic cathedrals are mingled with thoughts of Cairo, Damascus, and Cordoba, and one wonders how those restless alien stripes came to the hills of Tuscany.

H.V. Morton (1892-1979)

SIENA CATHEDRAL

When thoughts of sudden death appall you,
When a mist seems to cloud your days,
Then on the stones of the cathedral
Turn your exhausted, jaded eyes.

Roujou (1809-1876), A Street in Siena Victoria and Albert Museum Crown ©

Tell me, where dwells night everlasting?
Here, in this place. For, trembling, foaming,
The Sybil's lips in violent frenzy
Give warning of the Second Coming.

Accomplish your terrestrial business,
Accept your years, be satisfied.
Here, all over which we muse and ponder
Is captured by the chisel blade:

A little boy with bird and flower,
A man with scroll held in his hands,
And, at a tomb, on two sticks leaning,
Head bowed, a doddering ancient stands.

Be silent, soul. Don't touch or torture,
Don't summon, don't compel or bind:
The hour of love, stern, clear as crystal,
Shall come for certain in the end.

Alexander Blok (1880-1921)

IN A FIELD OF SIENA

Young girl that in the field hast work begun,
And with thy great straw hat dost seem the Sun,
Fair thief-of-hearts they call thee, every one.

Folk Rhyme

SIENA

The sun had set, all that tawny barren world seemed burning in the
conflagration of the ruined sun. The city flamed like some beautiful
beacon. Then suddenly, out of the fire, the bells of the Duomo rang the
message of the Angel. Swiftly, hysterically almost, with the eagerness of
a woman, the convent of S. Girolamo answered. From Santo Spirito,
from San Domenico, from San Martino, from Sant' Agostino, Santa
Mustiola, from San Francesco, over the city of the Virgin the bronze
voices mixed in a marvellous chorus singing Magnificat. The canticle

45

seemed to rise towering into the sky, like the bell-shaped, pure Lily of Annunciation. From the vineyards, from the gardens, from the cornfields, from the valleys and the hills came the soft country voices, bell answering bell, throbbing and beating, wave after wave, in an ever-widening circle of sound that broke at the feet of Siena, till at last their voices were lost in the silence that brooded over the valleys and the hills.

Again I looked out across that world, silent so suddenly, to Mont' Amiata, that in the failing light seemed infinitely far away, like a mountain in a dream. Ah, if I could reach her! There, why, there, if anywhere in the world, was all that I could desire, coolness and silence, the wind among the trees, and laughing streams bordered with forget-me-nots, and the little songs of the country, if I might trust Pio II. Why should I not set out?

One by one the cities faded in the twilight, little by little that barren world of hills was lost in an immense and beautiful shadow; out of Maremma night was coming, only Mont' Amiata, like a dim, vast precious stone, shone far away between earth and sky.

Why should I not set out?

Suddenly beneath me the olives stirred in the twilight, the corn whispered together and was silent, the dead grass on the wall, between the bricks, shivered and was still. There was a moment of profound stillness. Again the olives trembled, a swallow dipped past me crying plaintively; beside the church the dust curled up in little tongues like flames. It was the wind at last. At first it came in little gasps, like the cries of children; then with a flutter as of wings, like the flight of doves or the hurry of a girl's bare feet in the vineyard. Over the eastern hills the moon hung like the Host in a monstrance of jasper, the olives tossed their silver leaves as though in adoration, the corn was a sea of purple and gold, - it was the wind at last. And I heard a voice walking in the garden of the world like the voice of God.

When I looked again Mont' Amiata was lost in the night.

Edward Hutton (1875-1969)

Siena: The Palio

The Palio is a horse-race, which lasts about two minutes, thrice around the wide piazza. In those two mad minutes if your heart does not swell until it fills every cranny of your body, out to your eyes and your ears and your teeth, strangling all your guts in an orgasm of delight in the glory of man, sport, horses, colour, sun, the spilling, bubbling drunken wine of being alive in Italy, among a race that of all the races of the world best knows what it is to devour life not only to the last crumb and drop, but to the eating of the cups and plates as well - if this does not happen to you at the Palio, then you cannot know even the meaning of 'man', 'horse', or 'sun', let alone know how to enjoy them.

Only two minutes? But to those two minutes the build-up has been enormously elaborate. It has been going on, for the Sienese, for weeks beforehand, and on the day of the Palio the race itself is merely the climax to a scene of prolonged pageantry which, even without the race, is unique, delightful and exciting.

You must imagine you are sitting at the edge of a piazza of great extent, shaped like a mollusc-shell both as to its outline and its delicately hollowed centre, based on the town hall, surrounded by tall houses, rosy and serrated, with wooden stands beneath them, and every inch of space, except the track, black with a swaying mob of fifty thousand people. They stand jammed shoulder to shoulder on the square. They sit on the roofs. They bulge through the windows. They clamber up the poles. They crowd Jacopo della Quercia's lovely fountain. That dark sea is never at rest. Every so often there is a flurry: somebody has fainted, or someone is fighting. To-day, too, there is a faint, and unusual, threat of rain and the black sea keeps making little white blossoms of waves as faces lift to the sky. Otherwise we are all impatiently watching the clock tower and the far corner of the square. When, at last, the beginning of the procession appears and the great Sunta bell on top of the Mangia tower and all the bells of Siena begin to clang, and the multitude begin to roar, we know what the noise was like in the Roman amphitheatre when the first lions bounded in.

Group by group every parish appears, dressed in brilliant mediaeval costumes, carried so unselfconsciously that grace and realism are one. Each parish has its drummer, its captain, its men-at-arms, its horsemen, its recognisable standard, and its two flag-wavers who perform traditional and flawless agilities with their great coloured flags. They flap and wave them fluttering and crackling this way and that way, passing them under their elbows, behind their backs, in and out between their legs, ending up with the splendid trick called *sbandierata* when they throw them high in the air, like flaming torches, one to the other, while the audience roars frantic approval. I do not know how long this procession lasts; parish after parish; display after display; always the silver trumpets braying, the bells wildly clanging, the rising and falling cheers. Excitement never palls for a moment. By the time it has come to an end the mob is already worked-up to a pitch of delirium.

Sean O'Faolain (1900-)

The Palio in Siena is, of course, not a race at all in the true meaning of the word. It is a burlesque with a touch of cruelty about it which relates it to the comic races of the Italian Middle Ages and to the fist-fights of the period. Such races were held on feast days and were probably the most important part of the entertainment. Unlike the bloodstock races, which were held outside the town, the comic races were run through the streets. There were ass and buffalo races, races for Jews in Rome, in Milan for prostitutes, and in Florence for the old horses on which the dyers' boys loaded cloth to be washed in the Arno. There were even races for riderless horses. The animals had spikes attached to them, which drove them frantically through the streets between screens of canvas.

The French and Spanish invasions of the fifteenth century disrupted the racing of bloodstock, but new amusements arrived with the invaders. Under the Spaniards a form of bull-fight - *caccia di tori* - became popular in Siena and was held in the main piazza. Each contrada provided its bull, which was led round with each ceremony, and the contrada went to considerable trouble and expense to design a *macchina* or, as we should say today, a decorated float, into which the bull-fighters could retreat at moments of danger. This was the age of pageantry and triumphs, and the machines were ingenious and beautiful. When bull-fights were abolished in Tuscany in 1590, their place was taken during the annual festivals by a revival of the old burlesque races. To add a touch of splendour to them, the competing contrade organised a procession of cars, which were grander versions of the old *macchine*. It is from these cars that the seventeen contrade of Siena derive their puzzling names: The Tortoise, the Snail, the Wood, the Eagle, the Wave, the Panther, the Ram, the Tower, the Unicorn, the Owl, the Shell, the Dragon, the Goose, the Giraffe, the Caterpillar, the She-Wolf, and the Porcupine.

In true Renaissance fashion, most of the cars were classical tableaux or allegorical compositions. The car of the Dragon told the history of Cadmus. He was seen standing, spear in hand, upon a rocky landscape of canvas, having killed the dragon. As the float reached the grandstand, he extracted the dragon's teeth, which he cast about him, and wherever he threw them the canvas was agitated as an armed man sprang up. The car of the Goose represented the city of Rome being warned of the Gothic attack by the Capitoline geese. Roman soldiers were seen standing round battlements on which stood a goose, while Father Tiber reclined in a corner. The Giraffe car was a gilded enclosure in which the model of a gigantic and unusual girafe was attended by Moors: the animal's hide was white and its spots were red. The car of the Owl was an allegorical tableau which represented Wisdom and Intelligence. Its chief character was Minerva, who sat enthroned among classical deities while a boy walked in front holding a silver vase on which a live owl was perched.

A delightful car, which I should like to have seen, was that of the Caterpillar Contrada. It was escorted by gardeners wearing green jackets, yellow breeches, and bandoliers of flowers. Green and yellow ribbons fluttered from their hats and they carried a flag of yellow, green, and blue (the same colours are carried today), in the centre of which a green caterpillar stood upon a sprig of olive. This beautifully escorted car was a garden in the form of steps which led to an arched arbour and a fountain. As the car encircled the piazza, musicians seated upon the steps were heard playing their instruments.

H.V. Morton (1892-1979)

PORTOFERRAIO

The afternoon like dead skin; now heat bores
Relentlessly through shutters; you turn, half-pause
In combing salt out from your hair.
Outside, steps hesitate, continue on stone stair.
Beneath us, boats seem stuck over glass; walls
The colour of pollen crumble by water; a child calls.
The harbour looks oiled and heavy; lines of palms,
Dusty and grey, raise supplicating arms.
I watch you move against the mirror, beyond
The silver of your hairbrush see flies stalk
Across the bedspread; and when you talk
Our eyes meet in the glass, in the glass grow fond.

Beneath us, tissues of foam crinkling the limits of rock -
Salt crumbles where high walls shape this town like a heart.

Up here where the blue is propped by tamarisk
I use flat orange slabs like desks.

And note, as evidence, the ugliness of ore,
The pervading melancholy and drifts of chestnut.

Canes of watered green that swish like silk,
Mauve hills, and down below a fading sea.

Beaches are sand moors, but as dusk, fingering
An Emperor's things, in cool rooms, we're more

Conscious of gloom, stored ghosts like moths
Eating away history, siblings of power.

We squeeze this island like a grape, but later,
Conjugating winter, will spit out the husk, memory

Dry as a pip. Now there is only hardness of leaving,
This skyline writing out its name to remember.

Alan Ross (1922-)

CHAPTER 4
COUNTRY LANDSCAPES COUNTRY LIFE

Each shuttered room and every covered place,
Whatever they are made of, hold the night.
The day exists where the sun leaps and plays,
Distributing its full and generous light.

But if night can indeed be overcome
By fire or flame, even a glow-worm may
Conquer her as effectively as day;
One little light can break her powerful gloom.

The open land, where seeds and plants allow
The sun to give them light and life, can be
Broken and hurt by the encroaching plough.

Only in darkness can men fully be
Themselves, and therefore night is holier than
Day; no plant has half the worth of man.

Michelangelo (1475-1564)
Translated by Elizabeth Jennings (1970)

FROM THE PISAN CANTOS

no overstroke
no dolphin faster in moving
nor the flying azure of the wing'd fish under Zoagli
when he comes out into the air, living arrow.
and the clouds over the Pisan meadows
are indubitably as fine as any to be seen
from the peninsula
οỷ βάρ βάροι have not destroyed them
as they have Sigismundo's Temple
Divae Ixottae (and as to her effigy that was in Pisa?)
Ladder at swing jump as for a descent from the cross
O white-chested martin, God damn it,
as no one else will carry a message,
say to La Cara: amo.
Ezra Pound (1885-1972)

53

I found a house at Florence on the hill
Of Bellosguardo. 'Tis a tower which keeps
A post of double observation o'er
That valley of Arno (holding as a hand
The outspread city) straight toward Fiesole
And Mount Morello and the setting sun,
The Vallombrosan mountains opposite,
Which sunrise fills as full as crystal cups
Turned red to the brim because their wine is red.
No sun could die nor yet be born unseen
By dwellers at my villa: morn and eve
Were magnified before us in the pure
Illimitable space and pause of sky,
Intense as angels' garments blanched with God,
Less blue than radiant. From the outer wall
Of the garden, drops the mystic floating grey
Of olive trees (with interruptions green
From maize and vine), until 'tis caught and torn
Upon the abrupt black line of cypresses
Which signs the way to Florence. Beautiful
The city lies along the ample vale,
Cathedral, tower and palace, piazza and street,
The river trailing like a silver cord
Through all, and curling loosely, both before
And after, over the whole stretch of land
Sown whitely up and down its opposite slopes
With farms and villas.

Elizabeth Barrett Browning (1806-1861)

XXXVIII.

LOVE'S VAIN EXPENSE
Rendete a gli occhi miei

Give back unto mine eyes, ye fount and rill,
    Those streams, not yours, that are so full and strong,
    That swell your springs, and roll your waves along
    With force unwonted in your native hill!

And thou, dense air, weighed with my sighs so chill,
That hidest heaven's own light thick mists among,
Give back those sighs to my sad heart, nor wrong
My visual ray with the dark face of ill!

Let earth give back the footprints that I wore,
That the bare grass I spoiled may sprout again;
And Echo, now grown deaf, my cries return!

Loved eyes, unto mine eyes those looks restore,
And let me woo another not in vain,
Since how to please thee I shall never learn!

Michelangelo (1475-1564)
Translated by J. Addington Symonds (1878)

. . . and there was a smell of mint under the tent flaps
especially after the rain
and a white ox on the road toward Pisa
as if facing the tower,
dark sheep in the drill field and on wet days were clouds
in the mountain as if under the guard roosts.

Ezra Pound (1885-1972)

PASSAGE OF THE APENNINES - A FRAGMENT

Listen, listen, Mary mine,
To the whisper of the Apennine,
It bursts on the roof like the thunder's roar,
Or like the sea on a northern shore,
Heard in its raging ebb and flow
By the captives pent in the cave below.
The Apennine in the light of day
Is a mighty mountain dim and gray,
Which between the earth and sky doth lay;
But when night comes, a chaos dread

On the dim starlight then is spread,
And the Apennine walks abroad with the storm,
Shrouding...

Percy Bysshe Shelley (1792-1822)

At Sant' Antimo

Flanking the place,
a cypress
stretches itself, its surface
working as the wind
travels it in a continual
breathing, an underwater
floating of foliage
upwards, till
compact and wavering
it flexes a sinuous
tip that chases
its own shadow
to and fro
across the still
stone tower.

Charles Tomlinson (1927-)

Cypresses

Tuscan cypresses,
What is it?

Folded in like a dark thought
For which the language is lost,
Tuscan cypresses,
Is there a great secret?
Are our words no good?

The undeliverable secret,
Dead with a dead race and a dead speech, and yet

Darkly monumental in you,
Etruscan cypresses.

Ah, how I admire your fidelity,
Dark cypresses!

Is it the secret of the long-nosed Etruscans?
The long-nosed, sensitive-footed, subtly-smiling Etruscans,
Who made so little noise outside the cypress groves?

Among the sinuous, flame-tall cypresses
That swayed their length of darkness all around
Etruscan-dusky, wavering men of old Etruria:
Naked except for fanciful long shoes,
Going with insidious, half-smiling quietness
And some of Africa's imperturbable sang-froid
About a forgotten business.

What business, then?
Nay, tongues are dead, and words are hollow as hollow seed-pods,
Having shed their sound and finished all their echoing
Etruscan syllables,
That had the telling.

Yet more I see you darkly concentrate,
Tuscan cypresses,
On one old thought:
On one old slim imperishable thought, while you remain
Etruscan cypresses;
Dusky, slim marrow-thought of slender, flickering men of Etruria,
Whom Rome called vicious.

Vicious, dark cypresses:
Vicious, you supple, brooding, softly-swaying pillars of dark flame.
Monumental to a dead, dead race
Embalmed in you!

Were they then vicious, the slender, tender-footed,
Long-nosed men of Etruria?
Or was their way only evasive and different, dark, like cypress-trees in a
    wind?

They are dead, with all their vices,
And all that is left
Is the shadowy monomania of some cypresses
And tombs.

The smile, the subtle Etruscan smile still lurking
Within the tombs,
Etruscan cypresses.
He laughs longest who laughs last;
Nay, Leonardo only bungled the pure Etruscan smile.

What would I not give
To bring back the rare and orchid-like
Evil-yclept Etruscan?

For as to the evil
We have only Roman word for it,
Which I, being a little weary of Roman virtue,
Don't hang much weight on.

For oh, I know, in the dust where we have buried
The silenced races and all their abominations,
We have buried so much of the delicate magic of life.

There in the deeps
That churn the frankincense and ooze the myrrh,
Cypress shadowy,
Such an aroma of lost human life!

They say the fit survive,
But I invoke the spirits of the lost.
Those that have not survived, the darkly lost,
To bring their meaning back into life again,
Which they have taken away
And wrapt inviolable in soft cypress-trees,
Etruscan cypresses.

Evil, what is evil?
There is only one evil, to deny life
As Rome denied Etruria
And mechanical America Montezuma still.

D.H. Lawrence (1885-1930)

Edward Lear (1812-1888) The Tate Gallery, London
Above: San Miniato Al Monte, Florence, Below: Villa San Firenze, Florence

The heads, impenetrable
And the slow bulk
Soundless and stooping,
A white darkness - burdened
Only by sun, and not
By the matchwood yoke -
They groove in ease
The meadow through which they pace
Tractable. It is as if
Fresh from the escape,
They consent to submission,
The debris of captivity
Still clinging there
Unnoticed behind those backs:
'But we submit' - the tenor
Unambiguous in that stride
Of even confidence -
'Giving and not conceding
Your premises. Work
Is necessary, therefore -'
(With an unsevered motion
Holding the pauses
Between stride and stride)
'We will be useful
But we will not be swift: now
Follow us for your improvement
And at our pace.' This calm
Bred from this strength, and the reality
Broaching no such discussion,
The man will follow, each
As the other's servant
Content to remain content.

Charles Tomlinson (1927-)

SONNET CLVII

There stood a white doe on a meadow green
    Before me, with two golden horns displayed,

60

Betwixt two rivers, in a laurel's shade
At sunrise, when the air of spring was keen.
So winning and so stately was her mien,
That her to chase from every task I strayed;
So seeks a miser where his treasure's laid,
For trouble by delight is made serene.
Round her fair neck, 'To touch me none must dare,'
In diamonds and topazes was writ;
'My Caesar has been pleased to make me free.'
Then did the sun to turn at noon prepare;
My eyes were tired, but sated not a whit;
I got immersed, and out of sight was she.

Petrarch (1304-1374)
Translated by Cayley (1879)

To a Skylark

Shelley composed many of his greatest poems in Tuscany including
'Ode to the West Wind'. 'To a Skylark' was composed in Livorno in
1820.

Hail to thee, blithe Spirit!
Bird thou never wert,
That from Heaven, or near it,
Pourest thy full heart
In profuse strains of unpremeditated art.

Higher still and higher
From the earth thou springest
Like a cloud of fire;
The blue deep thou wingest,
And singing still dost soar, and soaring ever singest.

In the golden lightning
Of the sunken sun,
O'er which clouds are bright'ning,
Thou dost float and run;
Like an unbodied joy whose race is just begun.

The pale purple even
Melts around thy flight;
Like a star of Heaven,
In the broad daylight
Thou art unseen, but yet I hear thy shrill delight.

Keen as are the arrows
Of that silver sphere,
Whose intense lamp narrows
In the white dawn clear
Until we hardly see - we feel that it is there.

All the earth and air
With thy voice is loud,
As, when night is bare,
From one lonely cloud
The moon rains out her beams, and Heaven is overflowed.

What thou art we know not;
What is most like thee?
From rainbow clouds there flow not
Drops so bright to see
As from thy presence showers a rain of melody.

Like a Poet hidden
In the light of thought,
Singing hymns unbidden,
Till the world is wrought
To sympathy with hopes and fears it heeded not:

Like a high-born maiden
In a palace-tower,
Soothing her love-laden
Soul in secret hour
With music sweet as love, which overflows her bower:

Like a glow-worm golden
In a dell of dew,
Scattering unbeholden
Its aëreal hue
Among the flowers and grass, which screen it from the view!

Like a rose embowered
In its own green leaves,
By warm winds deflowered,
Till the scent it gives
Makes faint with too much sweet those heavy-wingèd thieves:

Sound of vernal showers
On the twinkling grass,
Rain-awakened flowers,
All that ever was
Joyous, and clear, and fresh, thy music doth surpass:

Teach us, Sprite or Bird,
What sweet thoughts are thine:
I have never heard
Praise of love or wine
That panted forth a flood of rapture so divine.

Chorus Hymeneal,
Or triumphal chant,
Matched with thine would be all
But an empty vaunt,
A thing wherein we feel there is some hidden want.

What objects are the fountains
Of thy happy strain?
What fields, or waves, or mountains?
What shapes of sky or plain?
What love of thine own kind? what ignorance of pain?

With thy clear keen joyance
Languor cannot be:
Shadow of annoyance
Never came near thee:
Thou lovest - but ne'er knew love's sad satiety.

Waking or asleep,
Thou of death must deem
Things more true and deep
Than we mortals dream,
Or how could thy notes flow in such a crystal stream?

We look before and after,
    And pine for what is not:
Our sincerest laughter
    With some pain is fraught;
Our sweetest songs are those that tell of saddest thought.

Yet if we could scorn
    Hate, and pride, and fear;
If we were things born
    Not to shed a tear,
I know not how thy joy we ever should come near.

Better than all measures
    Of delightful sound,
Better than all treasures
    That in books are found,
Thy skill to poet were, thou scorner of the ground!

Teach me half the gladness
    That thy brain must know,
Such harmonious madness
    From my lips would flow
The world should listen then - as I am listening now.

Percy Bysshe Shelley (1792-1822)

SHELLEY'S SKYLARK

Composed near Livorno in 1887

Somewhere afield here something lies
In Earth's oblivious eyeless trust
That moved a poet to prophecies -
A pinch of unseen, unguarded dust:

The dust of the lark that Shelley heard,
And made immortal through times to be; -
Though it only lived like another bird,
And knew not its immortality:

64

Lived its meek life; then, one day, fell -
A little ball of feather and bone;
And how it perished, when piped farewell,
And where it wastes, are alike unknown.

Maybe it rests in the loam I view,
Maybe it throbs in a myrtle's green,
Maybe it sleeps in the coming hue
Of a grape on the slopes of yon inland scene.

Go find it, faeries, go and find
That tiny pinch of priceless dust,
And bring a casket silver-lined,
And framed of gold that gems encrust;

And we will lay it safe therein,
And consecrate it to endless time;
For it inspired a bard to win
Ecstatic heights in thought and rhyme.

Thomas Hardy (1840-1928)

BAT

At evening, sitting on this terrace,
When the sun from the west, beyond Pisa, beyond the mountains of
   Carrara
Departs, and the world is taken by surprise . . .

When the tired flower of Florence is in gloom beneath the glowing
Brown hills surrounding . . .

When under the arches of the Ponte Vecchio
A green light enters against stream, flush from the west,
Against the current of obscure Arno . . .

Look up, and you will see things flying
Between the day and the night;
Swallows with spools of dark thread sewing the shadows together.

A circle swoop, and a quick parabola under the bridge arches
Where light pushes through;
A sudden turning upon itself of a thing in the air.
A dip to the water.

And you think:
'The swallows are flying so late!'

Swallows?

Dark air-life looping
Yet missing the pure loop . . . .
A twitch, a twitter, an elastic shudder in flight
And serrated wings against the sky,
Like a glove, a black glove thrown up at the light,
And falling back.

Never swallows!
Bats!
The swallows are gone.

At a wavering instant the swallows give way to bats
By the Ponte Vecchio . . .
Changing guard.

Bats, and an uneasy creeping in one's scalp
As the bats swoop overhead!
Flying madly.

Pipistrello!
Black piper on an infinitesimal pipe.
Little lumps that fly in air and have voices indefinite, wildly vindictive;

Wings like bits of umbrella.

Bats!

Creatures that hang themselves up like an old rag, to sleep;
And disgustingly upside down.
Hanging upside down like rows of disgusting old rags
And grinning in their sleep.

Bats!

In China the bat is symbol of happiness.

Not for me!

D.H. Lawrence (1885-1930)

Anonymous (16th century) Designs for ornamental panels   Victoria and Albert Museum Crown ©

CHAPTER 5

TURBULENT PAST

I have seen horsemen moving camp, and beating
   The muster and assault, seen troops advancing,
And sometimes with uncommon haste retreating.

Dante Alighieri (1265-1321)
Translated by Dorothy L. Sayers (1949)

GIOTTO'S CAMPANILE

Alone in the atoning belfry how I grieve
For all the motley, heroic and appalling
Soldiers who squander scraps of rationed leave

Within you, City: grieve, recalling
How Dante at what bitter distance bled.
Then, upon the spiral stair, steel heels falling,

The well-shod feet of the soon-to-be dead:
How casually they pause; note landmarks; curse the climb.
Hammers descend on the bronze above my head

To rivet us all to a pointless point in Time,
And over the town, trebles, twos and ones,
Shark-like shoals slip through the tidal chime,

Planes in flight, forming to swell the guns'
Staccato knell, tolling through acres of skies
For quivering loins and unengendered sons.

All sounds diminish, die. The far throb dies.
A grey sky waits for stars. No death is poured
Upon dim Florence, dusk-soft, drowsing in my eyes,

But bitterly, distantly, I bleed for the still adored

Now under terror and night - O vision city,
In all your campaniles which praised, implored,

None, none peals now, deep bells of love and pity.

Guy Butler (1918-)

71

O enslaved Italy, a place of grief,
A ship without a master in a great storm,
Not mistress of provinces, but a brothel!

Wretched country, look around your shores,
On every coast, and then into your heart
And see if any part enjoys peace.

Dante Alighieri (1265-1321)
Translated by C.H. Sisson (1980)

How the Parties of the Guelfs and Ghibellines Arose in Florence

For many years Tuscany was torn apart by the wars between the Guelfs and the Ghibellines. These struggles were a combination of the squabbles between different families and communes and the old recurring power struggle between Papacy and Empire. The Guelfs (to whom Dante belonged) were for the Pope and based mainly in Florence while the Ghibelline power was spread round other major towns. Often the towns themselves were divided and would change hands frequently.

In the year of Christ 1215, M. Gherardo Orlandi being Podestà in Florence, one M. Bondelmonte dei Bondelmonti, a noble citizen of Florence, had promised to take to wife a maiden of the house of the Amidei, honourable and noble citizens; and afterwards as the said M. Bondelmonte, who was very charming and a good horseman, was riding through the city, a lady of the house of the Donati called to him, reproaching him as to the lady to whom he was betrothed, that she was not beautiful or worthy of him, and saying: 'I have kept this my daughter for you;' whom she showed to him, and she was most beautiful; and immediately by the inspiration of the devil he was so taken by her, that he was betrothed and wedded to her, for which thing the kinsfolk of the first betrothed lady, being assembled together, and grieving over the shame which M. Bondelmonte had done to them, were filled with the accursed indignation, whereby the city of Florence was destroyed and divided. For many houses of the nobles swore together to bring shame upon the said M. Bondelmonte, in revenge for these wrongs. And being in council among themselves, after what fashion they should punish him, whether by beating or killing, Mosca de Lamberti said the evil word: 'Thing done has an end'; to wit, that he should be slain; and so it was done, for on the morning of Easter of the Resurrection the Amidei of San Stefano assembled in their house, and the said M. Bondelmonte coming from Oltrarno, nobly arrayed in new white apparel, and upon a white palfrey, arriving at the foot of the Ponte Vecchio on this side, just at the foot of the pillar where was the statue of Mars, the said M. Bondelmonte was dragged from his horse by Schiatta degli Uberti and by Mosca Lamberti and Lambertuccio degli Amidei assaulted and smitten, and by Oderigo Fifanti his veins were opened and he was brought to his end; and there was with them one of the counts of Gangalandi. For the which thing the city rose in arms and tumult; and this death of M. Bondelmonte was the cause and beginning of the accursed parties of Guelfs and Ghibellines in Florence, albeit long before there were factions among the noble citizens and the said parties existed by reason of the strifes and questions between the Church and the Empire; but by reason of the death of the said M. Bondelmonte all the families of the nobles and the other citizens of Florence were divided, and some held with the Bondelmonti, who took the side of the Guelfs, and were its leaders, and some with the Uberti, who were the leaders of the Ghibellines, whence followed much evil and disaster to our city, as hereafter shall be told; and it is believed that it will never have an end, if God do not cut it short. And surely it shows that the enemy of the human race, for the sins of the Florentines, had power in that idol of Mars, which the pagan Florentines of old were wont to worship, that at the foot of his statue such a murder was committed, whence so much evil followed to the city of Florence.

Giovanni Villani (1300-1348) Translated by R. Selfe (1906)

THE BATTTLE OF CAMPALDINO

. . . as it pleased God, the Florentines had the victory, and the Aretines were routed and discomfited, and between horse and foot more than 1,700 were slain, and more than 2,000 taken, whereof many of the best were smuggled away, some for friendship, some in return for ransom; but there came of them bound to Florence more than 740. Among the dead left on the field were M. Guiglielmino of the Ubertini, bishop of Arezzo, the which was a great warrior, and M. Guiglielmino de Pazzi of Valdarno and his nephews, the which was the best and the most

73

experienced captain of war that there was in Italy in his time; and there died there Bonconte, son of Count Guido of Montefeltro . . .

Giovanni Villani (1300-1348) Translated by R. Selfe (1906)

DANTE 3. BUONCONTE

'No one prays for me... Giovanna or the others.'
What took you so far from Campaldino
we never found your body? 'Where the Archiano
at the base of the Casentino loses its name
and becomes the Arno, I stopped running,
the war lost, and wounded in the throat -
flying on foot and splashing the field with blood.
There I lost sight and speech, and died saying *Maria*. . . .
I'll tell you the truth, tell it to the living,
an angel and devil fought with claws for my soul:
You angel, why do you rob me for his last word?
The rain fell, then the hail, my body froze,
until the raging Archiano snatched me,
and loosened my arms I'd folded like the cross.'

Robert Lowell (1917-1977)

Guicciardini the Florentine historian and statesman was employed both by the Papacy and the Medici for his wisdom.

I always maintain it to be more surprising that the Florentines should have acquired the scanty territory they possess, than that the Venetians or any other of the Italian powers should have gained their more extended dominions. For everywhere throughout Tuscany, even in its smallest towns, liberty had taken so strong a hold, that all were enemies to the aggrandisement of Florence. It is otherwise where you are surrounded by peoples used to servitude; for to these it matters so little whether they be ruled by one lord or by another, that they are never roused to any permanent or stubborn resistance. Besides which, we have, and always have had, a formidable obstacle to our growth in the nearness of the Church, who, from the depth to which she has struck her roots, has greatly hindered the spread of our dominion.

Francesco Guicciardini (1483-1540) Translated by N.Hill Thomson (1890)

'Whose bread and cheese I eat, to his tune I dance.'

Florentine saying

UGOLINO 1288

... the Pisans which had put in prison Count Ugolino and his two sons, and two sons of Count Guelfo, his son, as we before made mention, in a tower on the Piazza degli Anziani, caused the door of the said tower to be locked, and the keys thrown into the Arno, and refused to the said prisoners any food, which in a few days died there of hunger.

Giovanni Villani (1300-1348) Translated by R. Selfe (1906)

UGOLINO

'Others will pine as I pined in that jail
Which is called Hunger after me, and watch
As I watched through a narrow hole
Moon after moon, bright and somnambulant,
Pass overhead, until that night I dreamt
The bad dream and my future's veil was rent.
I saw a wolf-hunt; this man rode the hill
Between Pisa and Lucca, hounding down
The wolf and wolf-cubs. He was lordly and masterful,
His pack in keen condition, his company
Deployed ahead of him, Gualandi
And Sismundi as well and Lanfranchi,
Who soon wore down wolf-father and wolf-sons
And my hallucination
Was all sharp teeth and bleeding flanks ripped open.
When I awoke before the dawn, my head
Swam with cries of my sons who slept in tears
Beside me there, crying out for bread.
(If your sympathy has not already started
At all that my heart was foresuffering
And if you are not crying, you are hardhearted.)

They were awake now, it was near the time
For food to be brought in as usual,

75

Each one of them disturbed after his dream,
When I heard the door being nailed and hammered
Shut, far down in the nightmare tower.
I stared in my sons' faces and spoke no word.
My eyes were dry and my heart was stony.
They cried and my little Anselm said,
"What's wrong? Why are you staring, daddy?"
But I shed no tears, I made no reply
All through that day, all through the night that followed
Until another sun blushed in the sky
And sent a small beam probing the distress
Inside those prison walls. Then when I saw
The image of my face in their four faces
I bit on my two hands in desperation
And they, since they thought hunger drove me to it,
Rose up suddenly in agitation
Saying, "Father, it will greatly ease our pain
If you eat us instead, and you who dressed us
In this sad flesh undress us here again."
So then I calmed myself to keep them calm.
We hushed. That day and the next stole past us
And earth seemed hardened against me and them.
For four days we let the silence gather.
Then, throwing himself flat in front of me,
Gaddo said, "Why don't you help me, father?"
He died like that, and surely as you see
Me here, one by one I saw my three
Drop dead during the fifth day and the sixth day
Until I saw no more. Searching, blinded
For two days I groped over them and called them.
Then hunger killed where grief had only wounded.'
When he had said all this, his eyes rolled
And his teeth, like a dog's teeth clamping round a bone,
Bit into the skull and again took hold.

Seamus Heaney (1939-) from Dante's Divine Comedy

PISA

Fair Arno, while to me the mournful sound
Of vespers floats from the Pisan bells,

Above: William Blake (1757-1827), Dante and Virgil penetrating the Forest
The Tate Gallery London
Below: P. Pacini (c.1508), from Frederico Frezzi's Quadriregio

And turn by turn my contemplation dwells
On silent hills and shores with quiet crowned,

My heart with thousand thoughts of glory swells -
Thine ancient glories which through Time resound,
When thine ensanguined tide ran blood, renowned
Through discords of the Tuscan citadels.

When I compare those first and loftier days
Of souls austere and true, to what I see
In this dull age that laughs, disdains, delays;

Better, I cry, thy movement fierce and free,
Than this vile tedium of our baser ways,
O free and fortunate Thirteenth Century!

Enrico Panzacchi (1840-1904)
Translated by G.A. Greene (1893)

FLORENCE

How many times, in the years that you remember,
Have you changed laws and coinage, offices, customs,
And even brought in new inhabitants!
And if you see yourself in a clear light,
You will see that you resemble a sick woman
Who cannot stay quiet upon her bed
But twists and turns all the time to ease her pain.

Dante Alighieri (1265-1321)
Translated by C.H. Sisson (1980)

Pope Leo told me that his father, Lorenzo de Medici, would often say,
'Be sure that he who speaks evil of us does not wish us well.'

Francesco Guicciardini (1483-1540)
Translated by N. Hill Thomson (1890)

Pistoia was notorious throughout Tuscany, and particularly in Florence, for her ferocious blood feuds and treachery.

VI

I have received your word now twenty times,
Read it as many. May it do you good.
As little, I hope, as teeth can do for food
When stomach aches and indigestion climbs.

Now I know certainly that evil Cain
Was your own ancestor. You do again
What he and all his followers did. What good
They had has gone with your ingratitude.

Proud you are, envious, enemies of heaven,
Friends to your own harm and, to your own neighbour,
The simplest charity you find a labour.

See, to Pistoia Dante's curse was given.
Remember that if good words you say
Of Florence, you but wish to wheedle me.

A jewel far beyond all price is she.
This is a thing you cannot comprehend:
It takes real virtue thus to understand.

Michelangelo (1475-1564)
Translated by Elizabeth Jennings (1961)

PLAGUE

In the year then of our Lord 1348, there happened at Florence, the finest city in all Italy, a most terrible plague; which, whether owing to the influence of the planets, or that it was sent from God as a just punishment for our sins, had broken out some years before in the Levant; and after passing from place to place, and making incredible havoc all the way, had now reached the west; where spite of all the means that art and human foresight could suggest, as keeping the city clean from filth, and excluding all suspected persons; notwithstanding frequent consultations what else was to be done; nor omitting prayers to God in frequent processions: in the spring of the foregoing year, it began to shew itself in a sad and wonderful manner; and, different from what it had been in the east, where bleeding from the nose is the fatal prognostic, here there appeared certain tumours in the groin, or under the arm-pits, some as big as a small apple, others as an egg; and afterwards purple spots in most parts of the body: in some cases large and but few in number, in others less and more numerous, both sorts the usual messengers of death. To the cure of this malady, neither medical knowledge nor the power of drugs was of any effect; whether because the disease was in its own nature mortal, or that the physicians (the number of whom, taking quacks and women pretenders into the account, was grown very great) could form no just idea of the cause, nor consequently ground a true method of cure; whichever was the reason, few or none escaped; but they generally died the third day from the first appearance of the symptoms, without a fever or other bad circumstance attending. And the disease, by being communicated from the sick to the well, seemed daily to get a-head, and to rage the more, as fire will do by laying on fresh combustibles. Nor was it given by conversing with only, or coming near the sick, but even by touching their clothes, or anything that they had before touched. It is wonderful what I am going to mention; which, had I not seen it with my own eyes, and were there not many witnesses to attest it besides myself, I should never venture to relate, however credibly I might have been informed about it: such, I say, was the quality of the pestilential matter, as to pass not only from man to man, but, what is more strange and has been often known, that anything belonging to the infected, if touched by any other creature, would certainly infect, and even kill that creature in a short space of time: and one instance of this kind I took particular notice of, namely, that the rags of a poor man just dead, being thrown into the street, and two hogs coming by at the same time and rooting amongst them, and shaking them about in their mouths, in less than an hour turned round and died on the spot. These accidents, and others of the like sort, occasioned various fears and devices amongst those people that survived, all tending to the same uncharitable and cruel end; which was to avoid the sick, and everything that had been near them; expecting by that means to save themselves. And some holding it best to live temperately, and to avoid excesses of all kinds, made parties, and shut themselves up from the rest of the world; eating and drinking moderately of the best, and diverting themselves with music, and such other entertainments as they might have within doors; never listening to anything from without, to make them uneasy. Others maintained free living to be a better preservative, and would baulk no passion or appetite they wished to gratify, drinking and revelling incessantly from tavern to tavern, or in private houses; which were frequently found deserted by the owners, and therefore common to everyone; yet avoiding, with all this irregularity, to come near the infected.

Giovanni Boccaccio (1313-1375)
Translated by Manni (1874)

PLAGUE

From a letter from Ser Lapo Mazzei to Francesco Datini in 1400

I have seen two of my children (he wrote on 6 August) the oldest and the middle one, die in my arms, in a few hours. God knows how great my hopes were for the eldest, who was already my companion, and a father, with me, to the others. And how well he had got on in Ardingo's firm!...and God knows that, for many years, he never failed to say his daily prayers, in the morning and the evening on his knees in his room, so that often I pitied him, in the cold or heat. And God knows, and saw, how he behaved when he died: what counsels he gave, and how he said he was called to judgement, and was ready to obey . . . And in the same hour Antonia was sick to death, and in the same bed with her the second boy, who died beside her. Imagine how my heart broke, as I heard the little one weeping, and their mother not strong, and I heard the words of the eldest. Think of it: three dead! . . .

Francesco, take courage and trust in God and fear not; for if you put your hopes in Him, He will not fail you. Comfort your wife and she you; and loosen your spirit a little from these temporary possessions, and hold to God, and rest against His pillar, and you will never be confounded . . .

By God, do not write to Prato to collect money from your debtors. I was grieved, for your honour's sake, when I heard of it a few days ago. There is a time to chastise, and one to forgive.

Commend me to Monna Margherita. I commend my family to you, if I, too, should have to leave this mockery of life, for indeed it is a mockery, and there is little difference between life and death. Christ help you, and turn His intentions to our good.

Ser Lapo Mazzei (1350?-1412)
Translated by Iris Origo (1963)

FLOOD

In the year of Christ 1333, in the Calends of November, the city of Florence, being in great prosperity and in a happy and good condition, better than she had been since the year 1300, thanks to God, as, by the mouth of Christ, says his Evangelist Vigilate, for you know not the hour of the Judgment of God, which was sent on our city; when at the Ognissanti (All Souls) commenced the rain for Florence and all the surrounding country, and on the Alps, and the mountains; and this continued for four days and four nights, the rain increasing in an unusual manner, so that the cataracts of the sky appeared to have been opened; and with this rain continued frequent and frightful thunder and lightning, and the lightning fell sufficiently often. Therefore all people lived in great fear, ringing continually the bells of the city that the water might not rise; and in each house basins and buckets were used, and great cries circulated to God for mercy on those in peril, the inmates of the houses fleeing from roof to roof, making bridges of the buildings; and the noise and the tumult were so loud that the sound of the thunder was scarcely audible.

Giovanni Villani (1300-1348)
Translated by R. Selfe (1906)

Let no man scheme to make himself supreme in Florence who is not of the line of the Medici and backed besides by the power of the Church. None else, be he who he may, has such influence or following that he can hope to reach this height, unless indeed he be carried to it by the free voice of the people in search of a constitutional chief; as happened to Piero Soderini. If any therefore aspire to such honours, not being of the house of the Medici, let him affect the popular cause.

Francesco Guicciardini (1483-1540)
Translated by N. Hill Thomson (1890)

In 1473 Galeozzo Sforza, Duke of Milan agreed to sell Lorenzo de Medici Imola, a vital town on the trade route to Venice. However, Pope Sixtus IV wishing to found a new state for his nephew Girolamo Riario ordered the sale to be cancelled, buying Imola himself and dismissing the Medici as Papal bankers when they refused to grant him a loan. Girolamo, though, not content with Imola, wished to extend his territory without opposition from the Medici. He and the politically ambitious Francesco Pazzi, Lorenzo's replacement as Papal banker, decided with the Pope's agreement that the Medici family must be overthrown.

On Sunday, April 26, the Duomo was crowded. The Medici brothers were not seated but were strolling about, as Continental Catholics still do, chatting in low voices, ready to drop to one knee at certain moments. Contemporary writers do not agree on the precise point of the Mass selected by the murderers for their attack: some say it was the ringing of the sanctus bell: some the *Agnus Dei*, some the words, *Ite missa est.* Suddenly one of the murderers stabbed Giuliano and caused him to stumble against Francesco Pazzi, who began to attack him like a maniac, thrusting and stabbing so violently that he even managed to wound himself in the thigh. As Giuliano lay dead, one of the two priests, Antonio Maffei, a dagger in one hand, placed the other amateurishly upon the shoulder of Lorenzo de Medici in order to take better aim, with the result that Lorenzo shook him off and, drawing his sword and wrapping his cloak round his arm as a shield, vaulted over the lower wooden rail into the choir. Friends now surrounded him and together they ran through the crowd of frightened priests and choristers to the north sacristy, closing the heavy bronze doors (which are still there) in the face of the assassins. Though the gay Giuliano lay dead pierced by sixteen dagger wounds, Lorenzo was alive; and the Pazzi Conspiracy had failed.

How often some simple unexpected fact has wrecked the best laid plot. None of the conspirators knew that the Gonfalonier, an alert and suspicious magistrate called Cesare Petrucci, had recently fitted a self-locking device to the doors of the Palazzo Vecchio; so when, taking advantage of the confusion in the cathedral, those conspirators charged with the task of capturing the building entered it, they locked themselves in! They were easily overpowered, and were soon suspended from the windows of the Palace.

Botticelli was asked to paint upon the walls of the Palazzo Vecchio a picture showing them swinging there, but all trace of this work has long since vanished.

H.V. Morton (1892-1979)

A LETTER TO THE SIGNORIA

After the Pazzi conspiracy Pope Sixtus IV continued to undermine Lorenzo's power, finally declaring war on Florence and commanding King Ferrante of Naples to join him. After more than a year of fighting, when the enemy were only 30 miles from Florence, Lorenzo decided to risk Sixtus' aim of causing a revolution, leaving Florence and seeking peace in Naples with Ferrante. On leaving he wrote this letter to the Signoria.

Most illustrious Lords. If I did not inform you of the cause of my departure before I left Florence it was not from lack of respect, but because I held that the dangerous circumstances in which our city is placed demand action rather than deliberation. Peace it seems to me has become indispensable to us, and as all other means of obtaining it have become fruitless, I have chosen to expose myself to some degree of danger rather than to allow the city to suffer longer under its present trials. Therefore, with your permission, I propose to go directly to Naples. As I am the person against whom the attack of our enemies is chiefly directed, I may by delivering myself into their hands, be the means of restoring peace to my fellow-citizens. One of two things is certain. Either the King of Naples is friendly to us, as he has often stated and as some have believed, and is attempting in his attack to serve us rather than to rob us of our liberties, or he desires the ruin of the Republic. If his intentions are good there is no better way of putting them to the test than by placing myself unreservedly in his hands; this I venture to say is the only way of obtaining an honourable peace. If, on the other hand, the King's aim is the destruction of our liberties, it is best to know the worst at once, and to learn at the expense of one rather than of many. I am glad to be that one, firstly because I believe the principal object of hatred can more easily discover whether our enemies seek only to ruin me. Secondly, as I have had more honour and responsibility among you than my merits could claim, probably more than any private citizen has had in our day, I am more bound than any other person to serve my country, even at the risk of my life.

With this intention I now go. Perhaps God wills that this war, which began in the blood of my brother and of myself, should be ended by my means. My desire is that by my life or my death, my misfortunes or my prosperity, I may contribute to the welfare of our city. Should I be successful I shall rejoice in having won peace for my country and security for myself. Should I fail, I shall know that our misfortunes were necessary for our city's good; for if our adversaries aim only at me, they will have me in their power, and if they desire more it will be made plain. If need be, I know my fellow-citizens will unite in the defence of their liberty, and, by the favour of God, with the same success as our fathers have united in the past. I go full of hope, praying God to give me grace to perform what every citizen should be ready to perform for his country. I commend myself humbly to your Excellencies of the Signoria. Laurentius de Medici.

Lorenzo de Medici (1499-1492) Translated by C. M. Ady (1955)

LORENZO'S DEATH

The accurate representation of Lorenzo's death is neither as dramatic nor as bitter as this popular old version by Villari.

Lorenzo on that day was more conscious than he had yet been that his death was near at hand. He had called his son Pietro to him, and given him his parting advice, and had bid him a last farewell. When his friends, who were not allowed to be present at that interview, returned to the chamber, and had made his son retire, as his presence agitated Lorenzo too much, he expressed a wish to see Pico della Mirandola again, who immediately hastened to him. It appeared as if the sweet expression of the benevolent and gentle young man had soothed him a little, for he said to him, 'I should have died unhappy if I had not first been cheered by a sight of thy face'. Pico had no sooner retired than Savonarola entered, and approached respectfully the bed of the dying Lorenzo, who said there were three sins he wished to confess to him, and for which he asked absolution: the sacking of Volterra; the money taken from the *Monte delle Fanciulle,* which has caused so many deaths; and the bloodshed after the conspiracy of the Pazzi. While saying this he again became agitated, and Savonarola tried to calm him by frequently repeating, 'God is good, God is merciful!' Lorenzo had scarcely left off speaking, when Savonarola added, 'Three things are required of you.' 'And what are they, father?' replied Lorenzo. Savonarola's countenance became grave, and, raising the fingers of his right hand, he thus began: 'First, it is necessary that you should have a full and lively faith in the mercy of God'. 'That I have most fully.' 'Secondly, it is necessary to restore that which you unjustly took away, or enjoin your sons to restore it for you.' This requirement appeared to cause him surprise and grief; however, with an effort, he gave his consent by a nod of his head. Savonarola then rose up, and while the dying prince shrank with terror upon his bed, the confessor seemed to rise above himself when saying, 'Lastly, you must restore liberty to the people of Florence.' His countenance was solemn, his voice almost terrible; his eyes, as if to read the answer, remained fixed intently on those of Lorenzo, who, collecting all the strength that nature had left him, turned his back on him scornfully, without uttering a word. And thus Savonarola left him without giving him absolution; and the Magnificent, lacerated by remorse, soon after breathed his last.

Pasquale Villari (1826-1917) Translated by Leonard Horner (1863)

CRUELTY AND PASSION; AND WHETHER IT IS BETTER TO BE LOVED THAN FEARED, OR THE REVERSE

Machiavelli's 'Il Principe' was written in 1513.

Taking others of the qualities I enumerated above, I say that a prince should want to have a reputation for compassion rather than for cruelty: nonetheless, he should be careful that he does not make bad use of compassion. Cesare Borgia was accounted cruel; nevertheless, this cruelty of his reformed the Romagna, brought it unity, and restored order and obedience. On reflection, it will be seen that there was more compassion in Cesare than in the Florentine people, who, to escape being called cruel, allowed Pistoia to be devastated. So a prince should not worry if he incurs reproach for his cruelty so long as he keeps his subjects united and loyal. By making an example or two he will prove more compassionate than those who, being too compassionate, allow disorders which lead to murder and rapine. These nearly always harm the whole community, whereas executions ordered by a prince only affect individuals.

Niccolò Machiavelli (1469-1527) Translated by G. Bull (1963)

In Florence he who has not the qualifications for becoming head of affairs were a fool to involve himself so far with any government as to peril his whole fortune or its success; since what he may gain is as nothing to what he may lose. Nor let any man incur the risk of exile. For since our city is not divided into factions like the Adorni and Fregosi of Genoa, none will come forward to take his part, and he will be forced to lie abroad without money or credit; nay, may be reduced to beg for a livelihood. Of which fate, to those who remember him, Bernardo Ruccellai will be a sufficient example. This consideration alone should teach us to temporise, and so to conduct ourselves towards the head of the state that he shall have no ground to suspect us or to treat us as enemies.

Francesco Guicciardini (1483-1540) Translated by N.Hill Thomson (1890)

PERCH'IO NON SPERO DI TORNAR GIÀ MAI

Exile was a fate which befell many Tuscans.

Because no hope is left me, Ballatetta,
Of return to Tuscany,
Light-foot go thou some fleet way
Unto my Lady straightway,
And out of courtesy
Great honour will she do thee.

Tidings thou bearest with thee sorrow-fain
Full of all grieving, overcast with fear.
On guard! Lest anyone see thee or hear,
Any who holds high nature in disdain,
For sure if so, to my increase of pain,
Thou wert made prisoner
And held afar from her;
Hereby new harms were given
Me and, after death even,
Dolour and griefs renewed.

Thou knowest, Ballatetta, that Death layeth
His hand upon me whom hath Life forsaken;
Thou knowest well how great a tumult swayeth

87

My heart at sound of her whom each sense crieth,
Till all my mournful body is so shaken
That I cannot endure here,
Would'st thou make service sure here?
Lead forth my soul with thee
(I pray thee earnestly.)
When it parts from my heart here.

Ah, Ballatetta, to thy friendliness,
I do give o'er this trembling soul's poor case.
Bring thou it there where her dear pity is,
And when thou hast found that Lady of all grace
Speak through thy sighs, my Ballad, with thy face
Low bowed, thy words in sum:
'Behold, thy servant is come
- This soul who would dwell with thee -
Asundered suddenly
From Him, Love's servitor.'

O smothered voice and weak that tak'st the road
Out from the weeping heart and dolorous,
Go, crying out my shatter'd mind's alarm,
Forth with my soul and this song piteous
Until thou find a lady of such charm,
So sweetly intelligent
That e'en thy sorrow is spent.
Take thy fast place before her.
And thou, Soul mine, adore her
Always, with all thy might.

Guido Cavalcanti (1255-1300)
Translated by Ezra Pound (1885-1972)

MACHIAVELLI IN EXILE

A man is watching down the sun. All day,
Exploring the stone sinew of the hills,
For his every predilection it has asked
A Roman reason of him. And he has tried
To give one, tied to a dwindling patrimony

88

And the pain of exile. His guileless guile,
Trusted by nobody, he is self-betrayed.

And yet, for all that, Borgia shall be praised
Who moved and, moving, saved by sudden action:
The Florentines, despite their words, will have
Faction and the blood that comes of faction:
The work of France and Spain others begin -
Let him who says so exercise his powers
With dice and backgammon at a country inn:

Where, for his day's companions, he must choose
Such men as endure history and not those
Who make it: with their shadows, magnified
And spread behind them, butcher, publican,
Miller, and baker quarrel at their cards,
And heights and hill-roads all around are filled
With voices of gods who do not know they're gods.

Nor are they, save for a trick of light and sound:
Their fate is bound by their own sleeping wills.
Though lateness shadows all that's left to do,
Tarde non furon mai grazie divine:
The sun that lit his mind now lights the page
At which he reads and words, hard-won, assuage
What chance and character have brought him to.

He enters that courtly ancient company
Of men whose reasons may be asked, and he,
Released from tedium, poverty, and threat,
Lives in the light of possibility:
Their words are warm with it, yet tempered by
The memory of its opposite, else too soon
Hopes are a mob that wrangle for the moon.

Adversity puts his own pen in hand,
First torture, then neglect bringing to bear
The style and vigilance which may perfect
A prince, that he whom history forsook
Should for no random principle forsake

Its truth's contingency, his last defeat
And victory, no battle, but a book.

C. Tomlinson (1927-)

A Favour

To Lorenzo de Medici, Il Magnifico:

Lorenzo mine. Have mercy. God well knows how and in what attitude I write to you. A chopping-board on my bed, whereon lies my paper, my arm bare with the sleeve rolled up, I am as a dead man laden with bricks, with a head like a big onion on an arid heap of capelline (vermicelli), I seem to be all east wind. With trembling voice and hands I write, Signor mine, because the sacristan of Or San Michele has just come to my bedside to tell me that the priest of my little church which Your Magnificence promised to me, is dead; it is at Empoli and worth twelve or fifteen florins a month, and there are no duties. Now being vacant, Lorenzo, my life and hope, I throw myself into your arms. I know not what to say. I have but my own mother wit and my tongue. Do not judge of me for the love of God by my writing, but by my affection, my need, and the straits in which I find myself. I commend myself to you as heartily as I can, and will not again molest you. No more, in haste, I am sweating as though I were harnessed to a wagon. God keep you in health and prosperity, and inspire you to do what is best for the salvation of my soul. April 1st, 1474. - Your Matteo Franco.

'Not most faithful servant, for as yet there is nothing in which I can be faithful.'

Matteo Franco (c.1474) Translated by Y. Maguire (1936)

Whoso in Florence would be well liked by the people, must avoid a name for ambition, nor betray, even in the most trivial matters of everyday life, any desire to appear greater, grander, or more refined than his fellows. For in a city which has its foundation in equality, and brims over with jealousy, every man must needs be odious who is suspected of wishing to stand on a different level from the rest, or to deviate from the common mode of living.

Francesco Guicciardini (1483-1540) Translated by N. Hill Thomson (1890)

To Piero

Lorenzo's advice to his eldest son was not heeded by Piero who had little of his father's sagacity.

'Take care to speak well, and naturally, not in a forced manner, and do not try to seem learned, but use sweet and grave words with everyone.

'When you are anywhere with the young men belonging to other embassies, behave gravely and properly and soberly to your equals, and do not try to precede your elders because you are my son, for you are not anything more than a Florentine citizen.

'I am sending you with Giovanni Tornabuoni, and you must obey him in all things, and not do anything without him, and with him you must behave modestly and pleasantly with all, especially with gravity. You must try all the harder to do these things because they are not natural to your age. For the honours and caresses which will be showered upon you will be very dangerous to you if you are not careful, and always remember who you are.'

Lorenzo de Medici (1449-1492) Translated by Y. Maguire (1936)

How a Prince Should Organise his Militia

A prince, therefore, should have no other object or thought, nor acquire skill in anything, except war, its organisation, and its discipline. The art of war is all that is expected of a ruler; and it is so useful that besides enabling hereditary princes to maintain their rule it frequently enables ordinary citizens to become rulers. On the other hand, we find that princes who have thought more of their pleasures than of arms have lost their states. The first way to lose your state is to neglect the art of war; the first way to win a state is to be skilled in the art of war.

Niccolò Machiavelli (1469-1527) Translated by G. Bull (1963)

The Rise of Fascism in Florence

Back to Florence. Back to school. Greek now as well as Latin. One afternoon the boy grew tired of studying at home and went out into the street. Although he saw no one about, once more he had the feeling of tension in the air, of uneasiness, fear and violence. Presently he heard distant shots and explosions, which seemed to come at first from San Frediano, the working-class district, later from the centre of the town. There were sounds of shots from revolvers, rifles, machine-guns. Every so often he heard the sharp explosion of a mortar shell echoed by the surrounding hills.

Bullets came whistling through the air and buried themselves in the wall of the house he lived in. The white plaster crumbled, leaving the bare, red bricks. The sky was dark and rain began to fall. The noise of firing died away. There was not a soul to be seen in the streets. An armoured car sped across the broad square in front of the city gate and disappeared towards the town's centre. The *Piazza del Duomo* was crowded, but not with the usual milling mass of people going about their business, passing on their way to or from work, stopping to rest or chat with friends. Everywhere small groups of people were talking excitedly. A white-faced peasant spoke in gasps, as though his emotions were choking him: 'But I saw him myself! He'd had his brains blown out!"

That day at least a dozen people had been killed by the black-shirts and many more wounded.

At school, too, there was tension. Strikes - which meant not going to school - had become customary. One day he went to a public meeting where a school-teacher was giving a loud harangue. 'She used to be a communist, and now she is a fascist,' he heard people say.

A class-mate explained to him one day how his mother, a war-widow, had high hopes of a man who was going to save Italy. This was the first time he heard the name of the future dictator mentioned. It sounded ridiculous, reminding one of a well-known bandit, Musolino, and of the epithet *'messicano'*. He could not quite understand what Italy needed to be saved from: the blackshirts were the men who went about killing people, so how could the leader of the blackshirts claim to be a saviour? The boy was not impressed by the reverence, almost adoration, with which the name of the future dictator was mentioned. His immediate reaction was one of aversion, perhaps because he felt the injustice of inequalities, so that servility towards higher-ups was as distasteful to him as arrogance towards the peasants, the fishermen and the poor who lived in the slums. Every day now the papers gave news of fresh outrages, of buildings burned to the ground, of men and women killed and wounded. Squads of young men in black shirts marched along singing, making their way back from exploits which they attempted only when, like Mustafa and his gang, they were certain that their enemy was out-numbered and that they were protected by a government made weak by its members' lack of sense of responsibility. There were no more red carnations or red neck-ties to be seen anywhere.

Massimo Salvadori (1936-) Translated by G. Salvadori-Paleotti (1958)

July 31st. 1944 - I Tatti

The terrace of this villa, facing the heights, hills and mountains that environ the vale of Florence southward and westward is like the dress circle of a theatre, Florence itself being the orchestra and the hills beyond the stage.

From this dress circle, by moonlight yesterday we enjoyed - not in a physiological but in the aesthetic sense of the verb - a marvellous spectacle accompanied with appropriate music. The music consisted of the growl, the rumble, the roll of cannon that sounded antiphonal. Visually it was more impressive still. A distant mountain flamed up like Vesuvius. From beyond the hills came flashes of light, fan or pyramid shaped. This spectacle, this music went on for hours. Just what it meant was beyond me, although my fellow-spectators interpreted it to their satisfaction.

I could not help being frivolous, and wondering what people would not pay for a seat in our dress circle: to see the same performance, if it were merely theatrical, and not fraught with tragic possibilities.

Tragic-minded must have been many of the hundred thousand who, before noon yesterday, had to evacuate their homes from both sides of the Arno.

People of all classes were seen waiting for their turn to lap up water in any kind of vessel, no matter how humble, from ground taps. Others carrying what they could with them, to provide for the most rudimentary necessities. Still others bringing away the sick on wheel-barrows.

Why? I cannot believe that the Germans mean to defend Florence house by house. It does look, however, as if their plan is to blow up the bridges including the Ponte Vecchio and the Ponte della Trinita. For my part, as I already have written, I could more easily forgive the destruction of any other building.

Bernard Berenson (1865-1959)

Florence, January 10th, 1945: It will be some time before the city's physical wounds are healed; it will take still longer for the scars of fascism to be obliterated.

Contacts with the Partisans in the Apennines are based here and in Viareggio. There are not enough planes for delivering supplies. Crossing the lines means increasing our losses. For front line operations the Fifth Army Command has had the good sense to rely on Partisan brigades whose record has been beyond praise. On the other side of the lines, the fascist Republic of Salo has sent two or three divisions reorganised by the Germans. Their numerical superiority gave the *repubblichini* some success at Christmas, south of Carrara, but they were soon checked, thanks mainly to the courage and initiative of the Partisan brigades. This is civil war, the worst of all wars.

Liaison officers who were with the Partisans at Montefiorino and in Garfagnana, tell of the intrepidity of the Partisans - they know how to fight and how to die. Though the Expiation is painful, the last eighteen months have seen the emergence of a group which will, I hope, provide the leaders of tomorrow. This war is frightful, but at least it is strengthening the Italian character; without it, the Italians would surely have sunk into a morass of low politics and intrigues - as was already happening with the disgraceful Brindisi government. Perhaps they will still sink into the morass, but there is now a hope of avoiding it.

The shock of the unexpected German offensive in Belgium is beginning to pass. In Florence, Siena and Caserta, the Allied Command has been seriously concerned - partly because of the lack of adequate Allied troops in Italy. If the Germans should be encouraged by their success in Belgium to attack unexpectedly in Italy, things might go badly. Ever since Italy has become a secondary front there has been scarcity of everything.

Massimo Salvadori (1936-) Translated by G. Salvadori-Paleotti (1958)

THE PROPHECY OF DANTE

I would have my Florence great and free:
Oh Florence! Florence! unto me thou wast
Like that Jerusalem which the Almighty He
Wept over, 'but thou wouldst not'; as the bird
Gathers its young, I would have gathered thee
Beneath a parent pinion, hadst thou heard

My voice; but as the adder, deaf and fierce,
Against the breast that cherish'd thee was stirr'd
Thy venom, and my state thou didst amerce,
And doom this body forfeit to the fire.

Dante Alighieri (1265-1321)
Translated by Lord Byron (1788-1824)

WAR IN VAL D'ORCIA

During the war the Origos took in refugee children at their Tuscan farm La Foce.

June 22nd

The day begins badly. During the first lull in the firing a tragic procession begins to struggle down to our cellar: those of our Tuscan farmers who, until then, have preferred to take shelter in the woods. All night they have been under fire, and their drawn, terrified faces bear witness to what they have been through. They thankfully take refuge in the cellar and the vat-room - old men, women and children - about sixty more people to shelter and feed. An old grandmother from a neighbouring farm is among them; half paralysed, with a weak heart, she has been dragged along by her son and daughter, and now collapses, utterly exhausted. The babies whimper from cold and hunger. The older children go and whisper to ours, frightening them with the tales that I have tried to spare them until now. We go up to the kitchen (since fortunately the lull still continues) and I produce hot barley-coffee and bread-and-milk, the keeper having succeeded in finding and milking the cows. The farmers' account of their nights in the woods is not such as to encourage us to try to get through to the Allied lines with the children, a plan which again, this morning, we had considered. Sporadic firing goes on all through the morning.

This glimpse of a tiny segment of the front increases my conviction of the wastefulness of this kind of warfare, the disproportion between the human suffering involved and the military results achieved. In the last five days I have seen Radicofani and Contignano destroyed, the countryside and farms studded with shell holes, girls raped, and human beings and cattle killed. Otherwise the events of the last week have had little enough effect upon either side; it is the civilians who have suffered.

Pollaiuolo (1432-1498), Battle of Naked Men (detail)   Uffizi Gallery (Photo Alinari)

The above reflections were written during a lull in the shelling, in the kitchen, while boiling some milk for the children. But, in the midst of them, a louder burst of shell-fire than any we had experienced brought me down to the cellar, where we turned on the gramophone and started songs with the children, and waited. 'Now,' we felt, 'it really is beginning.' It had already been evident for some hours that shells of larger calibre were now being used, and both Antonio and I (though fortunately no one else) realised that the cellar was by no means proof against them. After a while, in another slight lull, the door opened, and a German sergeant came in: space would at once be required, he said, in the cellar (already filled to overflowing) for some German Troops. A few minutes later an officer appeared: 'You must get out,' he said, 'and get the children away. You can't keep them here. And we need the cellar.' (That same morning we had again asked this officer what we should do with the children, and he had said emphatically, 'Stay on!') 'If you get out at once,' he added, 'you may be able to get out of range during this lull.' There followed a few minutes of considerable confusion. Antonio and I were besieged by a crowd of terrified people, asking when and where they should go, what they should take with them, what they should leave behind, and so on. We could only answer: 'At once. To Montepulciano or Chianciano, wherever you have friends. Take only what you can carry with you - the clothes on your back, and some food.' The babies were howling, and, with Donata in my arms, I couldn't help Schwester much, but we managed to pack a basket with the babies' food, and the pram with some of their clothes and nappies. I took a tiny case, which we had in the cellar, containing a change of underclothes for Antonio and me, a pair of shoes, some soap and eau de cologne and face powder, my clock and Giorgio's photographs; and that is all that we now possess. Each of the children carried his own coat and jersey. The grown-ups each carried a baby, or sack of bread. And so, in a long, straggling line, with the children clutching at our skirts, half walking, half running, we started off down the Chianciano road.

I did not think, then, that we should get all the children through safely. We had been warned to stick to the middle of the road, to avoid mines, and to keep spread out, so as not to attract the attention of Allied planes. German soldiers, working at mine-laying, looked up in astonishment as we passed. *'Du lieber Gott!'* What are those children still doing here?' Some corpses lay, uncovered, by the roadside. A German

Red Cross lorry came tearing up the hill, nearly running over us. And all the time the shells were falling, some nearer, some farther off, and the planes flew overhead. The children were very good, the older ones carrying whatever they could, the smaller ones stumbling along as fast as their small legs could carry them. Donata shouted with glee on Antonio's shoulder. No one cried except the tiny babies, but now and again there was a wail: 'I can't go so fast!' and someone would pick up that child for a few hundred yards. The sun was blazing overhead, the hill very steep, and none of us had had any food since early breakfast. But every stumbling, weary step was taking us farther away from the cellar, and from what was still to come.

When we got to the top of the hill before Chianciano we divided into two parties. Those who had friends in Chianciano went on there, the rest of us, sixty in all (of whom four were babies in arms, and twenty-eight others children) started across country towards Montepulciano. The road itself was, we knew, under continual shell-fire, but we hoped to be able to cut across to the Villa Bianca cross-roads. The first part went well, and when at last we had a ridge between us and La Foce, we called first halt. The children fell exhausted and thankful on the ground, only to rise again hastily, having sat down on an ant-hill. They made, indeed, much more fuss about the ants than about the shells.

The shelling seemed farther off, the mined path was behind us, and a peasant brought us glasses of water. Until then, there had been no moment in which to stop and think, but now we began to realise, with dismay, all that we had left behind. The people in the vat-room - had they been warned? No one knew, and we looked at each other in horror. Then at last Assunta remembered: 'Yes, she had seen the fattore go in to warn them.' But what they could do next it was difficult to imagine, for the old grandmother who was with them was unable to walk, and there were also several children. Probably they would merely hide in terror in a ditch. One could only pray that none of them would be killed.

And then there was Giorgio's body. We had hoped to bury him the night before, so that at least we could show his grave to his family when we are able to trace them, but the firing on the road to the cemetery prevented us from getting there. So we had to leave him in that little room, unburied.[1]

And then the dogs - they, too, had been forgotten. We fed them up to yesterday, but in the hurry of leaving we did not remember to go up to the kennels (five hundred yards away, and under shell fire) to fetch them. And poor Gambolino, the poodle, is terribly gun-shy. Even if he is not killed he will go almost mad with fear. It does not bear thinking of.

After a brief rest (too brief, but as long as we dared) we went on again - Antonio and the keeper, Porciani, taking the longer and more dangerous road, on which the pram could be pushed, and the rest of us scrambling along a rough track up and down steep gulleys. The children were getting very tired, but struggled manfully on, and we lifted them over the steepest places. Twice planes came hovering over us, and we all crouched down in a ditch. Then when we came out into the open cornland, beyond Pianoia, came the worst part of the journey. The shelling had begun again, and on the Montepulciano road, a few hundred yards below us, shells were bursting with a terrific din. The children were afraid to go on, but on we must. Some more planes came over, and we lay down for cover in the tall corn. I remember thinking at that moment, with Benedetta lying beside me and two other children clutching at my skirts: 'This can't be real - this isn't really happening.'

At last we reached a farm on the road, occupied by a German Red Cross unit, and there again we got some water and a short rest. But the officer came out and, hearing that it was a *Kinderheim,* gave us disconcerting advice: take refuge at once in the Capuchin convent on the hill, he said, and don't push on to Montepulciano. 'What is happening at La Foce to-day, will happen there to-morrow.' For a minute we hesitated, but the convent, we knew, had no food and no sort of shelter, so we decided to risk it and push on. From this point onwards, the Germans said, the road was safe, and so we took it, a long, straggling, foot-sore procession. Half an hour after we had passed, that very stretch of the road was shelled.

After four hours we got to San Biagio, at the foot of the Montepulciano hill, and there sat down in a ditch for a breather before the last pull. We were very tired now, and a dreadful thought came over us: 'What if the Braccis should have left?' 'What if we find no shelter here?' But as we sat there, a little group of Montepulciano citizens appeared, then yet another: they had seen us from the ramparts, and were coming down to meet us with open arms. Never was there a more touching welcome. Many of them were partisans; others were refugees themselves from the south whom we had helped; yet others old friends among the Montepulciano workmen. They shouldered the children and our packages, and in a triumphant procession, cheered by so much kindness, we climbed up the village street, Antonio at the head, with Donata on his shoulder. Bracci and his wife Margherita came out to meet us, the children were at once settled on cushions on the terrace, and the Montepulcianesi vied with each other in offering accommodation. Antonio and I acted as billeting officers. Three went to one house, four to another, and the Braccis nobly took in not only our whole family, but all the refugee children as well. The Braccis' mattresses and blankets, which had been walled up, were pulled out again and laid on the ground, the children (after a meal of bread and cheese) put to bed, and at last we were able to wash and rest. Only one child was the worse for the terrible experience: Rino, who had a touch of the sun and suddenly fainted. Benedetta (sharing a bed with me) woke up, when I came to bed, to say 'We've left the bangs behind at last, haven't we?' and then fell into a twelve hours' sleep.

We have left behind everything that we possess, but never in my life have I felt so rich and so thankful as looking down on all the children as they lay asleep. Whatever may happen tomorrow, to-night they are safe and sound!

[1] When we got home we found the room empty, and under the cypresses, a few yards away, a fresh grave with a rough cross, on which was written *Unbekannter Italianer* (Unknown Italian). It was many months before we were at last able to trace his family in Bergamo.

Iris Origo (1902-)

IN HIDING IN TUSCANY

August 25th 1944

A faint breeze sprang up yesterday after sunset, and clouds appeared. One hoped for a change in the weather, but this morning the sky was like a gem of purest ray serene.

I no longer mind the deafening, crashing, spluttering noise of the cannonading. It seems to signify no more than the serving of tennis balls.

October 1944

The pine-clad, cypress-studded hills above me, cobwebbed over with innumerable paths, my favourite haunts for nearly half a century, must now be untrodden ground. They have been sown by the Germans with mines, and wayfarers have lost their lives. Walks must be

limited to the highroad winding steeply past Vincigliata to the hill-top
above - a little arduous for my eighty years.

Bernard Berenson (1865-1959)

FLORENCE GARIBALDI DAY 1949

No streets what they say.
No lovers
In the via dell'Amorino,
No beauties
In the via delle Belle Donne.
Only
The lovely women
Silent on their shelves,
Flowers before them
Fixed by the lovers of Saints.

And no plenty-
The hands
Stretched out for farthings,
The boys
With imprisoned birds,
While the amorous
Touch
Through blind chinks.

The bridge:
And the jewels
A deception.
Still
Hands grasping
Till the fingers
Reach to the clouds
And pull down
Nightfall.

Death of a day,
The river fades
And the last bird

101

Moved homeward
In his hungry cage;
This
Fifth of June;
No flag
Concerned with these.

No days
As they call them.

Arthur Boyars (1925-)

A Placard on a Float of Corpses in a Florentine Carnival

Fummo già come vo'sete,
Vo'sarete come noi.
As you are, so once were we;
As we are, so you will be!

CHAPTER 6

TRAVELLERS

It has come, it has come again,
This lost blue world
That I have not seen for seven years,
And now there is no other earth, no world beside it.
O what I have missed, these seven eyeless summers,
For this is a blue world shut unto itself,
This trellis of wistaria, this blue fire falling;
Its leaves drop flame to every quarter of the winds,
But I lived seven years away and came not to it,
And now the flowers are sevenfold, their honey tongues
Loll like a million bells that quiver and don't ring,
Though the air all trembles and vibrates with them
Then, as now, this blueness was alive
With quick spangled comedies, quick turncoat rain,
That fell by the trellis and was dyed in that colour;
There was never such a heaping, such a deep piled fulness,
For the flowers lie on the pergola like snow disastered,
From some whirling cataclysm thrown and tumbled.
Let us sit in this cage of fire and think of it!
Why is no poetry so full as this,
But this is mortal with but a breath of life;
Nothing lives outside it, if you keep within,
You have seven days, and a table and a chair;
What else can you wish, you are no prisoner?
Why ever move away from here, there's nothing else;
But keep in this cage of fire and live inside it,
Be the salamander in this house of flame;
Look from its windows, see the world on fire.
But now comes the aftermath, the hollow empty bathos,
For this blue flower faded at the bat winged dusk,
It faded and went out into a lifeless nothing;
Nor even did the scent stay in this worse than death.

Sacheverell Sitwell (1897-)

HANNIBAL'S ADVANCE INTO ETRURIA

While the consul was occupied in these propitiatory ceremonies and also
in the enrolment of troops, information reached Hannibal that

Flaminius had arrived at Arretium, and he at once broke up his winter quarters. There were two routes into Etruria, both of which were pointed out to Hannibal; one was considerably longer than the other but a much better road; the shorter route, which he decided to take, passed through the marshes of the Arno, which was at the time in higher flood than usual. He ordered the Spaniards and Africans, the main strength of his veteran army, to lead, and they were to take their own baggage with them, so that, in case of a halt, they might have the necessary supplies; the Gauls were to follow so as to form the centre of the column; the cavalry were to march last, and Mago and his Numidian light horse were to close up the column, mainly to keep the Gauls up to the mark in case they fell out or came to a halt through the fatigue and exertion of so long a march, for as a nation they were unable to stand that kind of thing. Those in front followed wherever the guides led the way, through the deep and almost bottomless pools of water and though almost sucked in by the mud through which they were half-wading, half-swimming, still kept their ranks. The Gauls could neither recover themselves when they slipped nor when once down had they the strength to struggle out of the pools; depressed and hopeless they had no spirits left to keep up their bodily powers. Some dragged their worn-out limbs painfully along, others gave up the struggle and lay dying amongst the baggage animals which were lying about in all directions. What distressed them most of all was want of sleep, from which they had been suffering for four days and three nights. As everything was covered with water and they had not a dry spot on which to lay their wearied bodies, they piled up the baggage in the water and lay on the top, whilst some snatched a few minutes' needful rest by making couches of the heaps of baggage animals which were everywhere standing out of the water. Hannibal himself, whose eyes were affected by the changeable and inclement spring weather, rode upon the only surviving elephant so that he might be a little higher above water.

Titus Livius (59BC - AD17)
Translated by D. Spillars (1854)

RETURN TO FLORENCE

A theatre-sky, of navy blue, at night:
traffic of the night, it darts, it screams,
it is straight swifts of night with lighted
eyes: upwards I read on a new building's

106

Face, Here P.B. Shelley wrote
Ode to the West Wind. Your poet, no. Nor
mine, yet say *wind* as he will or *wind,*
oh, I say *willkommen, welcome, ben-*

Venuto, oh, *bienvenu;* and I - I am
here again, after fourteen years: I-you.
I-you shall in a minute see the Duomo's
domino sides enormous up into the night,

I-you shall past *our* latteria stroll-there,
that corner shop where, look - for your
sake - the kind man scented my hair. Soon
must Il Bianco come into view,

The Loggia lighted, Dante again in the night,
reading, on walls. I-you. Sleeping. To swifts
of morning tomorrow waking. Dead and to come,
oh, *welcome, willkommen, benvenuti,* oh, *bienvenus!*

Geoffrey Grigson (1905-)

LOST IN FLORENCE

How the fatigues and annoyances of travel fill one with bitter
prejudices sometimes! I might enter Florence under happier auspices
a month hence and find it all beautiful, all attractive. But I do not care
to think of it now, at all, nor of its roomy shops filled to the ceiling with
snowy marble and alabaster copies of all the celebrated sculptures in
Europe - copies so enchanting to the eye that I wonder how they can
really be shaped like the dingy petrified nightmares they are the
portraits of. I got lost in Florence at nine o'clock, one night, and staid
lost in that labyrinth of narrow streets and long rows of vast buildings
that look all alike, until toward three o'clock in the morning. It was a
pleasant night and at first there were a good many people abroad, and
there were cheerful lights about. Later, I grew accustomed to prowling
about mysterious drifts and tunnels and astonishing and interesting
myself with coming around corners expecting to find the hotel staring
me in the face, and not finding it doing anything of the kind. Later still,
I felt tired. I soon felt remarkably tired. But there was no one abroad,

107

now - not even a policeman. I walked till I was out of all patience, and very hot and thirsty. At last, somewhere after one o'clock, I came unexpectedly to one of the city gates. I knew then that I was very far from the hotel. The soldiers thought I wanted to leave the city, and they sprang up and barred the way with their muskets. I said: 'Hotel d'Europe!'

It was all the Italian I knew, and I was not certain whether that was Italian or French. The soldiers looked stupidly at each other and at me, and shook their heads and took me into custody. I said I wanted to go home. They did not understand me. They took me into the guard-house and searched me, but they found no sedition on me. They found a small piece of soap (we carry soap with us, now,) and I made them a present of it, seeing that they regarded it as a curiosity. I continued to say Hotel d'Europe, and they continued to shake their heads, until at last a young soldier nodding in the corner roused up and said something. He said he knew where the hotel was, I suppose, for the officer of the guard sent him away with me. We walked a hundred or a hundred and fifty miles, it appeared to me, and then *he* got lost. He turned this way and that, and finally gave it up and signified that he was going to spend the remainder of the morning trying to find the city gate again. At that moment it struck me that there was something familiar about the house over the way. It was the hotel!

It was a happy thing for me that there happened to be a soldier there that knew even as much as he did; for they say that the policy of the government is to change the soldiery from one place to another constantly and from country to city, so that they cannot become acquainted with the people and grow lax in their duties, and enter into plots and conspiracies with friends. My experiences of Florence were chiefly unpleasant. I will change the subject.

Mark Twain (1835-1910)

THE STUART PALAZZO

A large and rambling old palazzo with stone balconies, many windows, and a railed-in courtyard stands at the corner of the Via Gino Capponi, not far from S.Annunziata. From certain positions on the pavement you can see an iron vane on the roof in the form of a flag, and with a pair of field-glasses you might be able to make out that the flag is pierced in the form of the letters 'C.R.' and the date '1777'. The letters stand for 'Carolus Rex' and the date is the year in which Bonnie Prince Charlie bought the house, which incidentally has the distinction of being the only property ever owned by the Stuarts during more than a century of exile.

As the owners of the house were not in Florence, I had to be content with a glimpse of the outside, and a conversation with a delightful old retainer who might have stepped out of some seventeenth century print. He was one of the most courteous watch-dogs I have ever met, and while we were talking I glanced into the entrance hall and saw, emblazoned in fresco upon the walls, the complex Royal Arms of Stuart England. Someone told me later that another relic of Charles Edward exists in a small room frescoed, incredible as it sounds, in Royal Stuart tartan.

The palazzo is the most interesting relic of the Stuarts in Italy. Charles halted his unhappy wandering life for a few years when, at the age of fifty-seven, he settled there with his lively young wife, Louise of Stolberg. He was already a mass of nerves and grievances and far gone in dissipation, and he bored Louise with rambling accounts of his adventures in the Highlands, and sometimes, when in his cups, was not responsible for his words or his actions. Outside the house, Charles and his wife were known as the Count and Countess of Albany; the moment they entered, and ascended the stairs beneath the Royal Arms, they became Charles III and his consort; and every detail of royal etiquette was observed. This was the period when Charles was spied on by Sir Horace Mann for the British Foreign Office.

Shortly after their arrival in Florence Louise met the handsome and charming young poet, Count Vittorio Alfieri, and they fell deeply in love. It was from this palazzo that she ran away from her husband's jealousy and the violence of his drinking bouts, eventually joining Alfieri, with whom she lived happily until his death some twenty years later.

Abandoned and still further humiliated, Charles Edward nevertheless managed to pull himself together and make one of the few successful decisions of his life. He asked his daughter, Charlotte, then in her thirties, to come and live with him in Florence. She was a devoted and charming woman, the child of his affair with Clementina Walkinshaw, whom he met during the '45, and she was able to recall her unhappy parent to a sense of his dignity, and to bring some happiness and tranquillity into the last three years of his life. Scotland remembers her as 'the bonnie lass of Albany.'

There is another building with Stuart memories in Florence, which, by some strange chance, remains in British occupation. This is the British Consulate in what used to be the *Casa Alfieri,* on the Lungarno Corsini. It was in this palazzo, after the death in Rome of Charles Edward, that Louise, Countess of Albany settled with her love. If anyone today wishes to have a visa on his passport or to have it renewed, the stamp will descend upon it in the little study where Alfieri once wrote his tragedies. Upstairs, the painted ceilings are those beneath which the Countess of Albany, called by some the Queen of England and, by others the Queen of Florence, held her famous *salon* in her old age attended by the whole of Florentine society and by every celebrated visitor to the city. After her poet's death she lost interest in her appearance, and some complained that she was dumpy and dowdy and her receptions boring, though they all accepted invitations to them. Her tomb in S. Croce bears above it the last lion and unicorn to support the armorial dignity of a Stuart sovereign.

H.V. Morton (1892-1979)

ENGLAND IN TUSCANY

Iris Origo spent much of her childhood at her mother's villa in Fiesole.

Sometimes, my grandparents came to Villa Medici to visit their daughter - Gran enjoying the house and garden and Gabba the walks and drives in the hills - but both of them a little bored by the constant intellectual and artistic talk, and trying to reassure themselves by repeating, 'But of course Sybil always did like this sort of thing!'

They brought England with them - but indeed England was already there. Florentine society at that time was not so much cosmopolitan as made up of singularly disparate elements - an archipelago of little islands that never merged into a continent. The worlds of the various colonies - Russian, French, German, Swiss, American and English - sometimes overlapped, but seldom fused and the English colony itself, though the largest and most prosperous, was far from being, in its own eyes, a single unit. 'They are, of course,' as E.M. Forster's clergyman delicately expressed it, 'not all equally... some are here for trade, for example.' The real gulf, however, lay not between one kind of resident and another, but between the mere tourist and the established Anglo-Florentine, who felt himself to have become as much part of the city life as any Tuscan. Some of these residents sank roots so deep that when, at

110

the outbreak of the Second World War, the British Consulate attempted to repatriate them, a number of obscure old ladies firmly refused to leave, saying that, after fifty years' residence in Florence, they preferred even the risk of a concentration camp to a return to England, where they no longer had any tie or home.

The English church in Via La Marmora, Maquay's Bank in Via Tornabuoni, Miss Penroses's school (where their children met all the little Florentines whose parents wished them to acquire fluent English), the Anglo-Amerian Stores in Via Cavour, Vieusseux's Lending Library and, for the young people, the Tennis Club at the Cascine - these were their focal points. If they lived in a Florentine *palazzo* it was at once transformed - in spite of its great stone fireplaces and brick or marble floors - into a drawing-room in South Kensington: chintz curtains, framed water-colours, silver rose-bowls and library books, a fragrance of home-made scones and of freshly made tea ('But no Italian will warm the tea-pot properly, my dear'). If they had a villa, though they scrupulously preserved the clipped box and cypress hedges of the formal Italian garden, they yet also introduced a note of home: a Dorothy Perkins rambling among the vines and the wisteria on the pergola, a herbaceous border on the lower terrace, and comfortable wicker chairs upon the lawns. *'Bisogna begonia!'* (the two words pronounced to rhyme with each other) I heard Mrs. Keppel cry, as, without bending her straight Edwardian back, she firmly prodded her alarmed Tuscan gardener with her long parasol, and then marked with it the precise spots in the beds where she wished the flowers to be planted. The next time we called, the begonias were there - as luxuriant and trim as in the beds of Sandringham.

Iris Origo (1902-)

Having seen all the curiosities of Florence, and hired a good travelling coach for seven weeks, at the price of seven zequines, something less than three guineas and a half, we set out post for Rome, by the way of Siena, where we lay the first night. The country through which we passed is mountainous, but agreeable. Of Siena I can say nothing from my own observation, but that we were indifferently lodged in a house that stunk like a privy, and fared wretchedly at supper. The city is large and well built: the inhabitants pique themselves upon their politeness, and the purity of their dialect. Certain it is, some strangers reside in this place on purpose to learn the best pronunciation of the Italian tongue. The Mosaic pavement of their duomo, or cathedral, has been much admired; as well as the history of Aeneas Sylvias, afterwards Pope Pius II, painted on the walls of the library, partly by Pietro Perugino, and partly by his pupil Raphael D'Urbino.

Next day at Buon Convento, where the emperor Henry VII, was poisoned by a friar with the sacramental wafer, I refused to give money to the hostler, who, in revenge, put two young unbroken stone-horses in the traces next to the coach, which became so unruly, that, before we had gone a quarter of a mile, they and the postillion were rolling in the dust. In this situaton they made such efforts to disengage themselves, and kicked with such violence, that I imagined the carriage and all our trunks would have been beaten in pieces. We leaped out of the coach, however, without sustaining any personal damage, except the fright; nor was any hurt done to the vehicle. But the horses were terribly bruised, and almost strangled before they could be disengaged. Exasperated at the villainy of the hostler, I resolved to make a complaint to the magistrate of the place, who is called *uffiziale*. I found him wrapped in an old, greasy, ragged, great coat, sitting in a wretched apartment, without either glass, paper, or boards in the windows; and there was no sort of furniture but a couple of broken chairs, and a miserable truckle bed. He looked pale, meagre, and haggard, and had more the air of a half-starved prisoner than of a magistrate. Having heard my complaint, he came forth into a kind of outward room or belfrey, and rung a great bell with his own hand. In consequence of this signal, the postmaster came up stairs, and I suppose he was the first man in the place, for the *uffiziale* stood before him cap in hand, and, with great marks of humble respect, repeated the complaint I had made. This man assured me, with an air of conscious importance, that he himself had ordered the hostler to supply me with those very horses, which were the best in his stable; and that the misfortune which happened was owing to the misconduct of the fore postillion, who did not keep the fore horses to a proper speed proportioned to the mettle of the other two. As he took the affair upon himself, and I perceived had an ascendency over the magistrate, I contented myself with saying, I was certain the two horses had been put to the coach on purpose, either to hurt or frighten us: and that, since I could not have justice here, I would make a formal complaint to the British minister at Florence. In passing through the street to the coach, which was by this time furnished with fresh horses, I met the hostler, and would have caned him heartily; but, perceiving my intention, he took to his heels and vanished. Of all the people I have ever seen, the hostlers, postillions, and other fellows hanging about the post-houses in Italy, are the most greedy, impertinent, and provoking. Happy are those travellers who have phlegm enough to disregard their insolence and importunity: for this is not so disagreeable as their revenge is dangerous. An English gentleman at Florence told me, that one of those fellows whom he had struck for his impertinence, flew at him with a long knife, and he could hardly keep him at sword's point. All of them wear such knives, and are very apt to use them on the slightest provocation. But their open attacks are not so formidable as their premeditated schemes of revenge; in prosecution of which the Italians are equally treacherous and cruel.

Tobias Smollett (1721-1771)

HILLS OF TUSCANY

In Florence the spring was over and the heat had come. The carved palaces quivered like radiators in the sun. Hot blasts of air, as from kitchen stoves, moved through the streets laden with odours of meat and frying oil. In the cheaper cafés brick-faced British tourists sat swearing and counting their crumpled money. But from the tower of the Palazzo Vecchio one could look out across the roasting roofs of the city and see the rising hills around - vistas of vine and olive, cool blue and frosted silver; a series of diminishing horizons, jagged and sparkling, floating south like icebergs in the fresh clear air.

I'd had my fill of Florence, lovely but indigestible city. My eyes were choked with pictures and frescoes, all stamped one on top of the other, blurred, their colours running. I began to long for those cool uplands, that country air, for the dateless wild olive and the uncatalogued cuckoo. I decided to walk to Siena, some fifty miles to the south, along the old road through the Chianti hills.

So I packed a rucksack, rolled up a sleeping-bag, bought a map, and left the city in a pair of stout shoes. It was noon, but it might have been midnight. The sun was blinding and the streets deserted. I took the Via Chiantigiana and walked in a daze for two hours. At two o'clock I flopped in the town square of Grassina and ate my lunch - bread, wine, fruit, and a memorable ice-cream.

In the café shade sat a row of old men with short silver hair, squeaking at one another like crickets. Nearby stood a row of mules,

113

covered with wet sheets, and dozing. In a dry and rubbishy gutter the town idiot sat fishing with rod and line. Curly-haired children, with the gilded faces of angels, taunted him happily and baited his hook with orange peel. For some time I watched a procession of girls, in flaming red dresses, filling their kettles at the public tap. Then heavy with wine I staggered out of the town and slept for two hours on a bank of sage.

Through the late afternoon I walked six miles, climbing slowly into the hills. The road was white and deep with dust. The dust lifted like smoke on the evening wind and coated my hair and hands with tiny fragments of marble - marble of the Tuscan cities and their white cathedrals. The hedges were rimmed with dust and starred with jasmine and dog-roses, huge blossoms, heavy, dilating, fat as clotted cream, and bigger than any others I have ever seen. And at six o'clock rose the dog-rose moon huge and pure white in the daylight sky.

My bag grew heavy, and heavier as I climbed. But at last I reached the crest of the Campo dell'Ugolino and took a farewell look at the Florentine hills - classical backcloths slashed with cypresses, powdered with grape-bloom by the evening sun, and glittering with alabaster villas.

At last I felt I was on my way, I had reached the first of those magical horizons, and my feet were sound. Larks started up, and cuckoos called, and bright green lizards shot from stone to stone. Under the long evening shadows I entered Strada-in-Chianti, and marked it on my map.

Strada, strung out along its street, was cool and busy, engrossed in flashing needles. Groups of young girls sat on the pavements embroidering and making lace. Old men with sharp knives split withies as though they were flaying devils. Old women, toothlessly chewing, were plaiting straw hats with black and frenzied fingers. Only the young men were idle, squatting on their haunches outside the wine shop talking of football.

I had a meal here - spaghetti cooked with oil and butter, black wine of the village, and two fried eggs. The plump girl who served me leaned through the window and sang with voluptuous melancholy into the street. The street was full of swallows, diving low. The room was full of flies.

When I had finished, the girl helped me on with my rucksack, feeling the weight of it and puffing huge sighs of consolation through her wine-coloured lips. 'Why do you walk?' she asked. 'Are you German?' 'No,' said I. 'Then *why?*' she repeated, mystified. I hadn't the word, nor the heart, to answer her.

114

Now through the red of sunset I went out of the village to find a place to sleep. A wood or a ruin would do, and I walked three miles looking for it. An uneasy time, full of illusions of homelessness, as the daylight dies, and the rose-warm clouds go dull, like wet ashes, and I enter the dark country and am suddenly startled by the sight of my moon-thrown shadow walking beside me.

I found a wood at last and unpacked among the bushes. The ground was hard and covered with little stones and flowers. The air was thick with the scent of thyme and honeysuckle. I rolled myself up in my bag and tried to sleep.

I shall not forget that night - it was worse than lying in the heart of a modern city. The moon came up over the trees and shone into my face like a street-lamp. Then, as though at the turn of a switch, the whole countryside suddenly began to whirr and roar, to squeak and whistle. The expected silence of the night became a cacophony of bellowing frogs, blundering beetles, crickets and cuckoos, mosquitoes, mice, donkeys, dogs and nightingales. There was no sleep or peace till the sun rose, and then it was too late and I was too stiff.

Laurie Lee (1914-)

A LETTER FROM DOSTOEVSKY

Only some parts of Sicily and Algiers can touch Florence for heat. Well, and so it was as hot as hell, and we bore it like true Russians, who notoriously can bear anything. I may add that for the last six weeks of our stay there, we were very hard-up. We had not, it is true, to suffer actual privation in any respect, nor did we deny ourselves anything, but our abode was thoroughly uncomfortable. We had been obliged, for unforeseen reasons, to leave the house where we had spent the winter; while we were waiting for that money, we went to a family with whom we are friendly, and rented provisionally a tiny dwelling. But as the money delayed to come, we had to stay in that hole (where we caught two beastly tarantulas) three whole months.

Our windows gave on a market-square with arcades and splendid granite-pillars; in the square was a municipal fountain in the form of a gigantic bronze boar from whose throat the water flowed (it is a classic masterpiece of rare beauty). Well, now reflect that all those arcades and the masses of stone by which the whole square is surrounded, drank in and accumulated all the heat of the sun, and got as scorching as a stovepipe in a vapour-bath - and that was the atmosphere we had to live in. The real heat that is, the real hell-heat, we had to groan under for six weeks (earlier, it was just in a sort of way endurable); it was nearly always 34 and 35 degrees Reaumur in the shade. You must know that the air, despite this heat and drought (it never once rained), was wonderfully light; the green in the gardens (of which there are astonishingly few in Florence; one sees hardly anything but stones) - the green neither withered nor faded, but seemed brighter and fresher every day; the flowers and lemon-trees had apparently only waited for the heat; but what astonished me most - me, who was imprisoned in Florence by untoward circumstances - was that the itinerant foreigners (who are nearly all very rich) mostly remained in Florence; new ones even arrived every day. Usually the tourists of all Europe throng, at the beginning of the hot weather to the German spas. When I saw in the streets well-dressed Englishwomen and even Frenchwomen, I could not conceive why these people, *who had money to get away with*, could voluntarily stay in such a hell. I was sorriest of all for poor Anya. The poor thing was then in her seventh or eighth month, and so suffered dreadfully from the heat. Moreover, the population of Florence spends the whole night on its feet, and there's a terrible deal of singing. Of course we had our windows open at night; then about five o'clock in the morning, the people began to racket in the market, and the donkeys to bray, so that we never could close an eye.

F. Dostoevsky (1821-1881)
Translated by E. E. Mayne (1917)

'We came back through Florence and the spectacle of that second rate provincial town with its repulsive Gothic architecture and its acres of Christmas card primitives made me almost sick. The only points about Florence are the country outside it, the Michelangelo tombs, Brunelleschi's dome and a few rare pictures. The rest is simply dung when compared to Rome. The Florentine country is, of course, as good as anything in the world; but the town...pooh.'

After a third-rate provincial town, colonised by English sodomites and middle aged lesbians, which is after all, what Florence is, a genuine metropolis (Rome) will be lively.'

Aldous Huxley (1894-1963)

116

In May 1947 Dylan Thomas arrived in Florence for the summer.

Villa del Beccaro,
Mosciano,
Scandicci.
Florence
May 20th 1947

My dear Margaret,

At last we've found, in pinewoods on the hills above Florence, a house until the end of July. The pooled ponded rosed goldfished arboured lizarded swinghung towelled winetabled Aeronshrill garden leads into our own (dear God) olives and vines climbing to a mutes' conventicle, a Niobe's eisteddfod, of cypresses. What seem to be armoured belligerent emerald wasps bang and bully the bushes; one-noted birds blow their brains out in the pines; other very near birds, which I can see, birdily fox me with very distant cries from the wrong trees. I can smell the sun. There is a swimming pool into which I have been only once - by mistake. Caitlin, Brigit, and the children are seals and newts there. Masciano, the nearest village, is thin and tall, shouldered like Peter Quennel against the church. (The Marquis of Q I met in Rome. He was spending a week with the British Ambassador, drinking, by the gallon, grappa, which, to me, tastes like an axe). Florence sparkles at night below us. In the day we see the Dome. It is perhaps five miles away. To get to the city we suffer by trap and tram. But there's so little need to move. The pine hills are endless, the cypresses at the hilltop tell one all about the length of death, the woods are deep as love and full of goats, the house is cool and large, the children beastly, the wine ample, why should I move at all until July the 31st. And then to the lovely unfound house in Oxfordshire, the house built round the desk you bought me? Oh I do hope so. And thank you thank you for the desk.

Did you receive the postcard, overcheerily scribbled with messages, after a big red dinner, by Caitlin, Natasha, Stephen and myself? Stephen was very gay, Natasha British as a hockeystick: I hadn't seen her like that. In flatheeled shoes she thumped the hot Florence pavements, gawky as an Arthur Marshall schoolgirl, shouting English, elbowing the droll Florentines from her gym-knickered way. I have met many of the young intellectuals of Florence, who are rarified and damp: they do not write much but oh how they edit! They live with

117

their mothers, ride motor-scooters, and translate Apollinaire.

And thank you, so very much indeed, for the books and papers which came to Rapallo and which were terribly welcome, all of them, Sunday papers, thrillers, Listeners. And for your lovely letter and for all it said. Do, do write again, and soon. Tell me all your news.

I wish I had heard you read my poems, and Vernon's, and Alun Lewis's, and Roy's 'Skull in the Desert'. I wish I had heard you reading, on the Macedonian lake, from my orange stamp-book. And the changing fish and the living fossils of that deepest legendary water! God's pulling your leg.

It is all so widely quiet here, and the valley vining away to the church towers. In the next room, in her rest hour, Aeronwy is singing an obscene song. Brigit's Tobias, a spotty frog-boy, is screaming in the lavatory. Llewelyn, in the garden, is trying to cut a boat out of a pinecone with a breadknife and has several fingers left. Brigit is superintending the screaming of the boy-frog. Caitlin has shut herself away and is learning Italian - undoubtedly by looking through the window at the trees. I am sitting in a half-shuttered room over the vineyard, writing to you who are in Oxford, and thanking you for everything always, and sending my love.

Write soon.

I read anything in English.

Yours ever,
Dylan.

By July, Thomas missed his friends and was feeling the heat.

To T. W. Earp

Villa del Beccaro,
Mosciano,
Scandicci,
Florence
July 11th 1947

My dear Tommy,
                In a shuttered room I roast
                Like a pumpkin in a serra
                And the sun like buttered toast
                Drips upon the classic terra,
                Upon swimming pool and pillar,

118

> Loggia, lemon, pineclad pico,
> And this quite enchanting villa
> That isn't worth a fico,
> Upon terrace and frutteto
> Of this almost a palazzo
> Where the people talk potato
> And the weather drives me pazzo—

I am awfully sick of it here, on the beautiful hills above Florence, drinking chianti in our marble shanty, sick of vini and contadini and bambini, and sicker still when I go, bumpy with mosquito bites, to Florence itself, which is a gruelling museum. I loved it in Rome, felt like Oppenheim on the Riviera, but we have been here, in this villa, two months and I can write only early in the morning, when I don't get up, and in the evening, when I go out. I've wanted to write to you, and have longed for a letter from you. We're coming back, some brown as shit, some bleached albino, one limp and carmine, all broke, early in August. Will you be in London, or visiting? I do hope we see each other often this autumn. I am told the bitter's better, and I will be writing a filmscript to buy same. We really do have an enormous swimming pool, (into which I have been only once, by mistake), and our own vineyard, olives, mosquitoes, and small Italian mice with blue chins. I have written a longish poem which I'd like to send you when it is typed by an Italian professor of English in Florence. I asked the professor about Elba, where we thought of going, and he said - it was the first remark I heard him make - 'Plenty di fish-dog'. He translates Henry James and Virginia Woolf. Give my love to May and yourself. Write when you can, before August if possible, and tell me where, if you're in London, as you said, last time we met, you might be, I can write. Now I am going out to the cicadas to shake my legs a bit.

> In the very opposite of haste,
> Dylan

Dylan Thomas (1914-53)

THE FLORENTINE

This tale was told to Italo Calvino by an old woman of Pisa. It shows the misery of the Florentine who has nothing to boast of and longs to travel.

There was once a Florentine who went out every evening into society and listened to the talk of the people who had travelled and seen something of the world. He never had anything to tell them, however, for he'd never been away from Florence a day in his life and therefore felt like a perfect blockhead.

He was thus filled with the urge to travel and knew no peace until he had sold all his belongings, packed his bags, and set out. He walked all day long and at dusk requested shelter for the night at the house of a priest. The priest invited him to supper and inquired, as they ate, the reason for the man's journey. Upon learning that the Florentine was travelling solely to come back to Florence with something to talk about, he said, 'I, too, have often had such a desire. If you like, we can travel together.'

'Fine', said the Florentine. 'I'd never dreamed I'd be so lucky as to have a travelling companion.'

The next morning they set out together, the Florentine and the priest.

At nightfall they came to a farm and requested shelter. The farmer asked, 'What is the purpose of your journey?' Hearing their account he, too, felt the urge to travel and left at daybreak with them.

The three had gone quite some distance, when they came to the palace of a giant. 'Let's knock on the door,' proposed the Florentine, 'so when we go back home we can tell about a giant.'

The giant answered the door himself and invited them in. 'If you'll stay with me,' he told them, once they were inside, 'I can certainly use a priest in the parish and a farmer on the farm. Although there is no practical need for a Florentine, a place can be found for him too.'

The three men talked the matter over. 'No doubt about it, working for a giant, we'd see some pretty unusual things. Goodness knows how much we'd have to talk about afterwards!' So they accepted his offer. He led them off to bed, with the understanding that the details would be worked out the next morning.

The next morning the giant said to the priest, 'Come and let me show you the parish records.' They went into a room and closed the door. The Florentine, who had a great deal of curiosity and feared that he might miss something interesting, put his eye to the keyhole. As the priest bent over the records, the giant raised his sword, cut off his head, and threw the remains through a trapdoor.

This will certainly be something to tell back in Florence! thought the Florentine. The only trouble is, people won't believe me when I tell them.

'I have put the priest where he belongs,' announced the giant. 'Now I'll look after the farmer. Come along and let me show you the records of the farm.'

Unsuspecting, the farmer followed the giant into that same room.

Through the keyhole the Florentine saw him bend over the records and the giant's sword come down on his neck. Then the farmer's remains went through the trapdoor.

The Florentine was gloating over how many extraordinary things he would now be able to tell back home, when it suddenly occured to him his turn would be next; in that case he wouldn't get to tell a single thing. More and more he felt like running away, when the giant emerged from the room and he said he would have lunch before looking after the Florentine. They sat down to the table, but the Florentine was thinking so hard about how to escape that he couldn't swallow a thing.

Now the giant had one eye that squinted. At the end of lunch, the Florentine spoke. 'What a pity! You are so handsome, but that eye there...'

The giant was ill at ease whenever anyone noticed that eye, and he began blinking, frowning, and squinting in his chair.

'I know of a herb,' continued the Florentine, 'which cures every eye disorder. I think I even saw some growing on the lawn of your park.'

'Really?' replied the giant. 'There's some right here at the palace? Let's go get it at once!'

He led him through the palace and onto the lawn, while the Florentine carefully noted where the keys were kept and how to get out when the time came to flee. On the lawn he picked a common weed. They went back inside, and he put it on to boil in a pot of oil.

'This is going to hurt very badly,' he told the giant. 'Can you stand the pain without moving a muscle?'

'Of course I can!' answered the giant.

'To make sure you keep perfectly still I'd better tie you to this marble table. If I don't, you'll be sure to move, and the operation will be a failure.'

As he was anxious to get that eye corrected, the giant consented to being tied to the marble table. When he was all bound up like a sausage, the Florentine poured the pot of boiling oil into his eyes, blinding him. Then in a flash he was down the steps, rejoicing to himself. 'This, too, will I relate.'

The giant let out a howl that shook the whole house, jumped up with the marble table bound to his back, and ran after the man as best he could. But realizing he would never catch him now, he fell back on a trick. 'Florentine!' he yelled. 'O Florentine! Why are you running away from me? Don't you want to finish the operation? How much will you take to finish it? Would you like this ring?' He threw him a ring. It was an enchanted ring.

'How about that!' said the Florentine. 'I'll take this back to Florence and show it to anybody who doesn't believe me!' But he'd no sooner picked it up and slipped it on than his finger turned to marble and weighted him completely to the ground. There he lay motionless, for the finger weighed tons and tons. He vainly tried to pull his finger out of the ring, but it stuck fast to him. The giant was almost upon him. At his wit's end, the Florentine pulled out his pocketknife and cut off the finger. That way he escaped and the giant caught him no more.

He reached Florence with his tongue hanging out, and gone forever was his urge not only to travel far and wide but also to talk about his journeys. As for the finger, he said he had cut it off mowing the grass.

Traditional - Retold by Italo Calvino (1923-)
Translated by George Martin (1980)

A ROMAN TRAVELLER

And now from Pisa's city turning back
To Triturrita, I to the fair South
The flapping sails was setting, when the sky,
With sudden rack o'ercast, grew foul with storm,
Flashed from the riven clouds their forked fires.
We stayed; for who beneath malignant storms
Would dare to journey through the furious waves?
Our rest from sailing in near woods we pass
And gladly ply our limbs in chase of game.
Our innkeeper provides the hunting-gear
And hounds the lair strong-scented trained to find.
By ambush and the snares of wide-meshed nets
The boar is slain, and falls - though terrible
For flashing tusks - a boar which Meleager
With shoulders strong would tremble to approach,
Which would relax the thews of Hercules.
Then through the echoing mountains rings the horn,
And the spoil's weight the hind makes light with song.

Rutilius Claudius Namatianus (late 4th - early 5th centuries)
Translated by George Savage Armstrong (1907).

When the Brownings arrived in Tuscany, with Wilson their maid, they quickly threw off the vestiges of their old sombre London life. Elizabeth in particular became a new person.

Now, for instance, instead of sipping a thimbleful of port and complaining of the headache, she tossed off a tumbler of Chianti and slept the sounder. There was a flowering branch of oranges on the dinner-table instead of one denuded, sour, yellow fruit. Then instead of driving in a barouche landau to Regent's Park she pulled on her thick boots and scrambled over rocks. Instead of sitting in a carriage and rumbling along Oxford Street, they rattled off in a ramshackle fly to the borders of a lake and looked at mountains; and when she was tired she did not hail another cab; she sat on a stone and watched the lizards. She delighted in the sun; she delighted in the cold. She threw pine logs from the Duke's forest on to the fire if it froze. They sat together in the crackling blaze and snuffed up the sharp, aromatic scent. She was never tired of praising Italy at the expense of England. '...our poor English', she exclaimed, 'want educating into gladness. They want refining not in the fire but in the sunshine.' Here in Italy was freedom and life and the joy that the sun breeds. One never saw men fighting, or heard them swearing; one never saw Italians drunk; - 'the faces of those men' in Shoreditch came again before her eyes. She was always comparing Pisa with London and saying how much she preferred Pisa. In the streets of Pisa pretty women could walk alone; great ladies first emptied their own slops and then went to Court 'in a blaze of undeniable glory'. Pisa with all its bells, its mongrels, its camels, its pine woods, was infinitely preferable to Wimpole Street and its mahogany doors and its shoulders of mutton. So Mrs. Browning every day, as she tossed off her Chianti and broke another orange from the branch, praised Italy and lamented poor, dull, damp, sunless, joyless, expensive, conventional England.

Wilson, it is true, for a time maintained her British balance. The memory of butlers and basements, of front doors and curtains, was not obliterated from her mind without an effort. She still had the conscience to walk out of a picture gallery 'struck back by the indecency of the Venus.' And later, when she was allowed, by the kindness of a friend, to peep through a door at the glories of the Grand Ducal Court, she still loyally upheld the superior glory of St. James's 'It...was all very shabby', she reported, 'in comparison with our English Court.' But even as she gazed, the superb figure of one of the Grand Duke's bodyguard caught her eye. Her fancy was fired; her judgment reeled; her standards toppled. Lily Wilson fell passionately in love with Signor Righi, the guardsman.

Virginia Woolf (1882-1941)

From a letter - August 11th 1849

...'Did you ever see this place, I wonder? The coolness, the charm of the mountains, whose very heart you seem to hear beating in the rush of the little river, the green silence of the chestnut forest, and the seclusion which anyone may make for himself by keeping clear of the valley villages; all these things drew us. Robert and I go out and lose ourselves in the woods and mountains, and sit by the waterfalls on the starry and moonlight nights... Robert is better, looking better, and in more healthy spirits, and we are both enjoying this great sea of mountains and our way of life here altogether.'

Elizabeth Barrett Browning (1806-1861)

A WRITER'S DIARY

Monday, May 15th

This should be all description - I mean of the little pointed green hills; and the white oxen and the poplars and the cypresses and the sculptured shaped infinitely musical, flushed green land from here to Abbazia – that is where we went today; and couldn't find it and asked one after another of the charming tired peasants, but none had been 4 miles beyond their range, until we came to the stonebreaker and he knew. He could not stop work to come with us, because the inspector was coming tomorrow. And he was alone, alone, all day with no one to talk to. So was the aged Maria at the Abbazia. And she mumbled and slipped her words, as she showed us into the huge bare stone building: mumbled and mumbled, about the English - how beautiful they were. Are you a Contessa she asked me. But she didn't like Italian country either. They seem stinted, dried up; like the grasshoppers and with the manners of impoverished gentle people; sad, wise, tolerant, humorous.

124

There was the man with the mule. He let the mule gallop away down the road. We are welcome, because we might talk; they draw round and discuss us after we've gone. Crowds of gentle kindly boys and girls always come about us and wave and touch their hats. And nobody looks at the view - except us - at the Euganean, bone white, this evening; then there's a ruddy red farm or two; and light islands swimming here and there in the sea of shadow - for it was very showery - then there are the black stripes of cypresses round the farm; like fur edges; and the poplars and the streams and the nightingales singing and sudden gusts of orange blossom; and white alabaster oxen with swinging chins - great flaps of white leather hanging under their noses - and infinite emptiness, loneliness, silence: never a new house, or a village; but only the vineyards and the olive trees, where they have always been. The hills go pale blue, washed very sharp and soft on the sky; hill after hill.

Virginia Woolf (1882-1941)

Alan Moorehead went to Tuscany to convalesce after the war. At first he was fascinated by her beauty and people (particularly Berenson) but after a while his feelings changed.

Presently I began to suffer from that dreadful ennui that must overtake all self-appointed exiles who live in beautiful places in the sun. One lovely day succeeded another, the outlook was always upon cypresses and flowers and olive groves, every village church and contadino's cottage was part of the even texture of the landscape and nothing was vile. One lived like a queen bee, cossetted and cherished, and all the world was honey. Had one been born and brought up in Florence things might have been different; then one would have had a share of responsibility for what was going on around one, and associations reaching back into the past. But as things were it mattered not in the least to me who won the local elections or whether the hail destroyed the grapes or whether or not Florence defeated Turin at football.

The manifest correction for this detachment was work, but it was not always possible to work, and by the end of the second year the usual distractions began to fall into a wearisome routine. One made a patience of living. Meeting the same people all the time conversation declined into gossip and good food became monotonous, and having seen the pictures in the Uffizi and the sunset light from San Miniato for the twentieth time one did not want to go to those places any more.

Even the enthusiasm of one's friends arriving from the bleak and ugly north was not enough to break up this log-jam of satiety, this sickly vacuity, this creeping paralysis in the soft air. 'Another bad day', runs an entry in my diary, 'with ennui only just held at bay by manufacturing a round of minor things to do. Time, Machiavelli says, drives everything before it. Not me.'

Berenson himself, I fancy also feared this emptiness; that is why he visited every church in Tuscany, he had written his books, he had built his villa, he had his library, his friends, his fame and his disciples; really did lie here, he had his roots. Fifty years or more ago, as a penniless young man he had gone over the frescoes in these Tuscan churches inch by inch, riding out each morning on his bicycle with his pocket full of candles to light the dusky corners, returning at night to write up his notes - and home then was a pensione on the Arno. He had visited every church in Tuscany, he had written his books, he had built his villa, he had his library, his friends, his fame and his disciples; Florence was where he had to be. But for me it did not really matter whether I was in Florence or not, I was perching here in a rented villa making a mental convalescence from the war, and there were times when, in an extremity of boredom, deserts of nothingness on every side, I would go over to I Tatti just to clutch my way back to life again, the faithful hound in search of his master's voice.

Alan Moorehead (1910-1983)

On The Road To Alvernia

St Francis of Assisi travelled with his brothers to Alvernia where he was to receive the Holy Stigmata - the wounds of Christ.

...thereafter, in the morning, because they knew that, by reason of the fatigue of the night which he had passed without sleep, St. Francis was very weak in body and could ill have travelled on foot, his companions went to a poor labourer of that district, and besought him for the love of God to lend his little ass to St. Francis, their father, who could not go on foot. Now, when this man heard them make mention of Friar Francis, he asked them: 'Are ye some of the friars of that friar of Assisi whereof so much good is spoken?' The friars answered 'Yes'; and that it was in truth for him that they asked the beast of burden. Then the good man made ready the little ass, with great devotion and diligence, and led it to St. Francis with great reverence and made him mount thereon; and they continued their journey; and he with them, behind his little ass. And, when they had gone some distnce, the villain said to St. Francis: 'Tell me, art thou Friar Francis of Assisi?' And St. Francis answered him, 'Yea.' 'Strive thou, then (said the villain), to be as good as all folk hold thee to be, for there are many which have great faith in thee; and therefore I admonish thee, that thou fall not short of that which men hope to find thee.' Hearing these words, St. Francis did not disdain to be admonished by a villain, and said not within himself: 'What beast is this that admonisheth me?' even as many proud fellows who wear the friar's habit would say to-day; but forthwith he cast himself to earth from the ass, and kneeled him down before the villain and kissed his feet, and thanked him humbly, because he had deigned to admonish him so charitably. Then the villain, together with the companions of St. Francis, raised him up from the ground with great devotion, and set him upon the ass again, and continued their journey.

The Little Flowers of St. Francis and his Friars (c. 1300)
Translated W. Heywood (1906)

Agostino Carracci (1557-1602), St. Francis Victoria and Albert Museum Crown ©

CHAPTER 7

THE ARTS

IN SANTA CROCE

LIV

In Santa Croce's holy precincts lie
Ashes which make it holier, dust which is
Even in itself an immortality,
Though there was nothing save the past, and
    this,
The particle of those sublimities
Which have relapsed to chaos; here repose
Angelo's, Alfieri's bones, and his,
The starry Galileo, with his woes;
Here Machiavelli's earth return'd to
    whence it rose.

LV

These are four minds, which, like the elements,
Might furnish forth creation: – Italy!
Time, which hath wrong'd thee with ten
    thousand rents
Of thine imperial garment, shall deny,
And hath denied, to every other sky,
Spirits which soar from ruin: thy decay
Is still impregnate with divinity,
Which gilds it with revivifying ray;
Such as the great of yore, Canova is to-day.

LVI

But where repose the all Etruscan three –
Dante, and Petrarch, and, scarce less than they,
The Bard of Prose, creative spirit! he
Of the Hundred Tales of love – where did they
    lay
Their bones, distinguish'd from our
    common clay
In death as life? Are they resolved to dust,
And have their country's marbles nought to say?
Could not her quarries furnish forth one bust?
Did they not to her breast their filial earth entrust?

LVII

Ungrateful Florence! Dante sleeps afar,
Like Scipio, buried by the upbraiding shore;
Thy factions, in their worse than civil war,
Proscribed the bard whose name for evermore
Their children's children would in vain adore
With the remorse of ages; and the crown
Which Petrarch's laureate brow supremely
    wore,
Upon a far and foreign soil had grown,
His life, his fame, his grave, though rifled –
    not thine own.

LVIII

Boccaccio to his parent earth bequeath'd
His dust, - and lies it not her great among,
With many a sweet and solemn requiem breathed
O'er him who form'd the Tuscan's siren tongue?
That music in itself, whose sounds are song,
The poetry of speech? No; – even his tomb
Uptorn, must bear the hyaena bigot's wrong,
No more amidst the meaner dead find room,
Nor claim a passing sigh, because it told for *whom*!

LIX

And Santa Croce wants their mighty dust;
Yet for this want more noted, as of yore
The Caesar's pageant, shorn of Brutus' bust,
Did but of Rome's best Son remind her more:
Happier Ravenna! on thy hoary shore,
Fortress of falling empire! honour'd sleeps
The immortal exile; – Arqua, too, her store
Of tuneful relics proudly claims and keeps,
While Florence vainly begs her banish'd
    dead and weeps.

Lord Byron (1788-1824)

Piero della Francesca (1410-1492), The Resurrection of Christ
Galleria Comunale San Sepolcro (Photo Alinari)

D. H. Lawrence thought The Resurrection at Borgo San Sepolcro 'the Most Beautiful Picture in the World'

This country God, who rises in the grey light while human beings are still asleep, has been worshipped ever since man first knew that the seed is not dead in the winter earth, but will force its way upwards through an iron crust. Later He will become a god of rejoicing, but His first emergence is painful and involuntary. He seems to be part of the dream which lies so heavily on the sleeping soldiers, and has himself the doomed and distant gaze of the somnambulist.

Kenneth Clark (1903-1983)

RESURRECTION

(By Piero degli Franceschi, at Borgo)

Sleep holds you, sons of war: you may not see
(You whose charmed heads sink heavy in your hands)
How 'twixt the budding and the barren tree
With glory in his staring eyes, he stands.
There's a sharp movement in this shivering morn
That blinds your senses while it breaks your power:
The Phoenix grips the eagle: Christ reborn
Bears high the standard. Sleep a little hour:
Sleep: it were best ye saw not those bright eyes
Prepared to wreck your world with errant flame,
And drive strong men to follow mysteries,
Voices, and winds, and things that have no name.
Dare you leave strength half-proved, duty half-done?
Awake! This God will hunt you from the sun!

James Elroy Flecker (1884-1915)

CIMABUE AND GIOTTO

Cimabue – Etruscan born; gave, we saw, the life of the Norman to the tradition of the Greek: eager action to holy contemplation. And what more is left for this favourite shepherd boy Giotto to do, than this, except to paint with ever-increasing skill? We fancy he only surpassed Cimabue – eclipsed by greater brightness.

Not so. The sudden and new applause of Italy would never have been won by mere increase of the already kindled light. Giotto had wholly another work to do. The meeting of the Norman race with the Byzantine is not merely that of action with repose – not merely that of war with religion, – it is the meeting of *domestic* life with *monastic,* and of practical household sense with unpractical Desert insanity.

I have no other word to use than this last. I use it reverently, meaning a very noble thing; I do not know how far I ought to say – even a divine thing. Decide that for yourselves. Compare the Northern farmer with St.Francis; the palm hardened by stubbing Thornaby waste, with the palm softened by the imagination of the wounds of Christ. To my own thoughts, both are divine: decide that for yourselves; but assuredly, and without possibility of other decision, one is, humanly speaking, health; the other unhealthy; one sane, the other – insane.

To reconcile Drama with Dream, Cimabue's task was comparatively an easy one. But to reconcile Sense with – I still use even this following word reverently – Non-sense, is not so easy; and he who did it, first, – no wonder he has a name in the world.

I must lean, however, still more distinctly on the word 'domestic'. For it is not Rationalism and commercial competition – Mr. Stuart Mill's 'other career for woman than that of wife and mother' – which are reconcilable, by Giotto, or by anybody else, with divine vision. But household wisdom, labour of love, toil upon earth according to the law of Heaven – *these* are reconcilable, in one code, of glory, with revelation in cave or island, with the endurance of desolate and loveless days, with the repose of folded hands that wait Heaven's time.

Domestic and Monastic. He was the first of Italians – the first of Christians – who *equally* knew the virtue of both lives, and who was able to show it in the sight of men of all ranks, – from the prince to the shepherd; and of all powers, – from the wisest philosopher to the simplest child.

...For, note the way in which the new gift of painting bequeathed to him by his great master, strengthened his hands. Before Cimabue, no beautiful rendering of human form was possible; and the rude or formal types of the Lombard and Byzantine, though they would serve in the tumult of the chase, or as the recognized symbols of creed, could not represent personal and domestic character. Faces with goggling

Giotto (1266-1336), Detail from frescoes in the Bardi Chapel, Santa Croce
Capp. Bardi, Santa Croce (Photo Alinari)

eyes and rigid lips might be endured with ready help of imagination, for gods, angels, saints, or hunters – or for anybody else in scenes of recognized legend; but would not serve for pleasant portraiture of one's own self – or of the incidents of gentle, actual life. And even Cimabue did not venture to leave the sphere of conventionally reverenced dignity. He still painted – though beautifully – only the Madonna, and the St. Joseph, and the Christ. These he made living, – Florence asked no more: and 'Credette Cimabue nella pintura tener lo campo.'

But Giotto came, from the field; and saw with his simple eyes a lowlier worth. And he painted – the Madonna, and St.Joseph, and the Christ, – yes, by all means, if you choose to call them so, but essentially, – Mamma, Papa, and the Baby. And all Italy threw up its cap, – 'Ora ha Giotto il grido.'

For he defines, explains, and exalts, every sweet incident of human nature; and makes dear to daily life every mystic imagination of natures greater than our own. He reconciles, while he intensifies, every virtue of domestic and monastic thought. He makes the simplest household duties sacred; and the highest religious passions, serviceable, and just.

John Ruskin (1819-1900)

GIOTTO

The son nodded. With a look of sombre satisfaction, he led the way to the Peruzzi Chapel. There was a hint of the teacher about him. She felt like a child in school who had answered a question rightly.

The chapel was already filled with an earnest congregation, and out of them rose the voice of the lecturer, directing them how to worship Giotto, not by tactile valuations, but by the standards of the spirit.

'Remember,' he was saying, 'the facts about this church of Santa Croce; how it was built by faith in the full fervour of medievalism, before any taint of the Renaissance had appeared. Observe how Giotto in these frescoes – now, unhappily, ruined by restoration – is untroubled by the snares of anatomy and perspective. Could anything be more majestic, more pathetic, beautiful, true? How little, we feel, avails knowledge and technical cleverness against a man who truly feels!'

'No!' exclaimed Mr Emerson, in much too loud a voice for church.

'Remember nothing of the sort! Built by faith indeed! That simply means the workmen weren't paid properly. And as for the frescoes, I see no truth in them. Look at that fat man in blue! He must weigh as much as I do, and he is shooting into the sky like an air-balloon.'

He was referring to the fresco of the Ascension of St John. Inside, the lecturer's voice faltered, as well it might. The audience shifted uneasily, and so did Lucy. She was sure that she ought not to be with these men; but they had cast a spell over her. They were so serious and so strange that she could not remember how to behave.

E.M.Forster (1879-1970)

LUCA SIGNORELLI: TO HIS SON

The son of the painter Luca Signorelli (1441? -1523) appears in many of his pictures.

They brought thy body back to me quite dead,
Just as thou hadst been stricken in the brawl.
I let no tear, I let no curses fall,
But signed to them to lay thee on the bed.

Then, with clenched teeth, I stripped thy clothes soaked red;
And taking up my pencil at God's call,
All night I drew thy features, drew them all,
And every beauty of thy pale chill head.

For I required the glory of thy limbs,
To lend it to archangel and to saint,
And of thy brow for brows with halo rims;

And thou shalt stand, in groups that I shall paint
Upon God's walls; till, like procession hymns
Lost in the distance, ages make them faint.

Eugene Lee-Hamilton (1845-1907)

FRA ANGELICO (1387-1445)

On reflection you may see that the painter's design, so far as coherent, has been simply to offer an immense representation of Pity, and all

Luca Signorelli (1441-1523), Detail of the Altarpiece of The Circumcision
National Gallery London

with such concentrated truth that his colours here seem dissolved in tears that drop and drop, however, softly, through all time. Of this single yearning consciousness the figures are admirably expressive. No later painter learned to render with deeper force than Fra Angelico the one state of the spirit he could conceive – a passionate pious tenderness. Immured in his quiet convent, he apparently never received an intelligible impression of evil; and his conception of human life was a perpetual sense of sacredly loving and being loved.

Henry James (1843-1916)

...But it is impossible to bestow too much praise on this holy father, who was so humble and modest in all he did and said and whose pictures were painted with such facility, and piety. In their bearing and expression, the saints painted by Fra Angelico come nearer to the truth than the figures done by any other artist. He would never retouch or correct his pictures, leaving them always just as they had been painted since that, as he used to say, was how God wanted them. It is also said that Fra Angelico would never take up his brushes without a prayer. Whenever he painted a Crucifixion the tears would stream down his face, and it is no wonder that the faces and attitudes of his figures express the depth and sincerity of his Christian piety.

Giorgio Vasari (1511-74) Translated by G. Bull (1965)

Fra Angelico is buried in Rome. On the marble is carved this epitaph.

Non mihi sit laude, quod eram velut alter Apelles,
Sed quod hucra tuis omnia, Christe, dabam:
Altera nam terris opera extant, altera coelo.
Urbs me Joannem flos tulit Etruriae.

In praise of me, O Lord, be it not said
That I did match Apelles, but that I
My wages to thy people gave entire;
For different are the deeds that count on earth
From those in heaven.
In that city was I, John, born
That is the flower of Tuscany.

Translated by G. Bull (1965)

*Engraving of Venus Reclining with Cupids after Botticelli (detail) (1442-93)
ascribed to del Sellaio*

From heaven he came, in mortal clothing, when
All that was worst and best had been observed.
Living, he came to view the God he served
To give the entire, true light again.

For the bright star which with its vivid rays
Picked out the humble place where I was born –
For this, the world would be a prize to scorn;
None but its Maker can return its praise.

I speak of Dante, he whose work was spurned
By the ungrateful crowd, those who can give
Praise only to the worthless. I would live

Happy were I but he, by such men scorned,
If, with his torments, I could also share
His greatness, both his joy and exile bear.

Michelangelo (1475-1564)
Translated by Elizabeth Jennings (1926-)

Venus Reclining by Jacopo del Sellaio (1442-1493).

THE PICTURE

The eyes of this dead lady speak to me,
For here was love, was not to be drowned out.
And here desire, not to be kissed away.
The eyes of this dead lady speak to me.

OF JACOPO DEL SELLAIO

This man knew out the secret ways of love,
No man could paint such things who did not know.

And now she's gone, who was his Cyprian,
And you are here, who are 'The Isles' to me.

And here's the thing that lasts the whole thing out:
The eyes of this dead lady speak to me.

Ezra Pound (1885-1972)

PIERO'S LA MADONNA DEL PARTO

She stands, *La Madonna del Parto,* within a little tent, in a stillness greater than mere lack of motion, between the soft, deep-red folds of the tent's opening. Time has faded and dulled the material, so that the burden of the two angels who hold these tented folds apart is as intangible as a cloud. She stands, her child within her, heavy beneath her heart, with her hand parting the worn blue dress above the great curve of her pregnancy.

I existed in the chapel, within the great orb and bubble of stillness which enlarged my little complacent cone of well-being, beyond places and circumstances. I heard only the sharp, panting breath of the little girl behind me, and gradually this painful breathing was somehow transferred to the Madonna. The lady seemed to breathe, and to breathe the more quickly than one should be allowed to see; I had no right to be present. I saw a pulse in her throat as I looked at her, standing in a womb of dust, against dust, waiting to give birth...in a cemetery.

I walked back through the door and out into the sun, and I saw three small dishevelled boys grouped among the gravestones. They were staring beyond me through an open door. For a moment I feared to look, and when I turned and looked back, I saw only the little girl arranging the battered flowers and placing on the altar a large and ornate cross she seemed to have found. The silver face still gazed gently down. 'È bella la donna' said one little boy, very quietly. 'eccola', said the second. I walked in the glittering heat towards the black iron gate and towards the town. As I left, *'Bella'*, repeated the third boy, in a whisper.

Michael Ayrton (1921-)

BOTTICELLI'S FORTEZZA

38. I promised, some note of Sandro's Fortitude, before whom I asked you to sit and read the end of my last letter; and I've lost my own

notes about her, and forget now, whether she has a sword, or a mace; – it does not matter. What is chiefly notable in her is – that you would not, if you had to guess who she was, take her for Fortitude at all. Everybody else's Fortitudes announce themselves clearly and proudly. They have tower-like shields, and lion-like helmets – and stand firm astride on their legs, – and are confidently ready for all comers.

Yes; – that is your common Fortitude. Very grand, though common. But not the highest, by any means.

Ready for all comers, and a match for them, – thinks the universal Fortitude; – no thanks to her for standing so steady, then!

But Botticelli's Fortitude is no match, it may be, for any that are coming. Worn, somewhat; and a little weary, instead of standing ready for all comers, she is sitting, – apparently in reverie, her fingers playing restlessly and idly – nay; I think – even nervously, about the hilt of her sword.

For her battle is not to begin to-day, nor did it begin yesterday. Many a morn and even have passed since it began; and now – is this to be the ending day of it? And if this – by what manner of end?

That is what Sandro's Fortitude is thinking, and the playing fingers about the sword-hilt would fain let it fall, if it might be: and yet, how swiftly and gladly will they close on it, when the far-off trumpet blows, which she will hear through all her reverie!

John Ruskin (1819-1900)

Filippo Lippi (1406-1469)

It is said that Fra Filippo was so lustful that he would give anything to enjoy a woman he wanted if he thought he could have his way; and if he couldn't buy what he wanted, then he would cool his passion by painting her portrait and reasoning with himself. His lust was so violent that when it took hold of him he could never concentrate on his work. And becasue of this, one time or other, when he was doing something for Cosimo de Medici in Cosimo's house, Cosimo had him locked in so that he wouldn't wander away and waste time. After he had been confined for a few days, Fra Filippo's amorous or rather his animal desires drove him one night to seize a pair of scissors, make a rope from his bed-sheets and escape through a window to pursue his own pleasures for days on end. When Cosimo discovered that he was gone, he searched for him and eventually got him back to work. And after that he always allowed him to come and go as he liked, having regretted the way he had shut him up before and realizing how dangerous it was for such a madman to be confined. Cosimo determined for the future to keep a hold on him by affection and kindness and, being served all the more readily, he used to say that artists of genius were to be treated with respect, not used as hacks.

In Prato near Florence, where he had some relations, Fra Filippo stayed for many months doing a great deal of work in various parts of the district in company with Fra Diamante of the Carmelite convent at Prato, who had been his companion when they were novices together. Subsequently, he was asked by the nuns to paint the altarpiece for the high altar of Santa Margherita, and it was when he was working at this that he one day caught sight of the daughter of Francesco Buti of Florence, who was living there as a novice or ward. Fra Filippo made advances to the girl, who was called Lucrezia and who was very beautiful and graceful, and he succeeded in persuading the nuns to let him use her as a model for the figure of Our Lady in his painting. This opportunity left him even more infatuated, and by various ways and means he managed to steal her from the nuns, taking her away on the very day that she was going to see the exposition of the Girdle of Our Lady, one of the great relics of Prato. This episode disgraced the nuns, and Francesco, the girl's father, never smiled again. He did all he could to get her back, but either from fear or some other reason she would never leave Fra Filippo; and by him she had a son, Filippo, who became, like his father, a famous and accomplished painter.

Giorgio Vasari (1511-1574)
Translated by G. Bull (1965)

AFTER THE DEATH OF VITTORIA COLONNA.
IRREPARABLE LOSS

Se'l mi rozzo martello.

When my rude hammer to the stubborn stone
  Gives human shape, now that, now this, at will
  Following his hand who wields and guides it still,

145

It moves upon another's feet alone:
But that which dwells in heaven, the world doth fill
    With beauty by pure motions of its own;
    And since tools fashion tools which else were none,
    Its life makes all that lives with living skill.
Now, for that every stroke excels the more
    The higher at the forge it doth ascend,
    Her soul that fashioned mine hath sought the skies
Wherefore unfinished I must meet my end,
    If God, the great artificer, denies
    That aid which was unique on earth before.

Michelangelo (1475-1564)
Translated by J. Addington Symonds (1840-1893).

THE VENUS DE MEDICI

   She is very beautiful; very satisfactory; and has a fresh and new charm about her, unreached by any cast or copy that I have seen. The hue of the marble is just so much mellowed by time as to do for her all that Gibson tries, or ought to try, to do for his statues by color; softening her, warming her almost imperceptibly, making her an inmate of the heart as well as a spiritual existence. I felt a kind of tenderness for her; an affection, not as if she were one woman, but all womankind in one. Her modest attitude – which, before I saw her, I had not liked, deeming that it might be an artificial shame – is partly what unmakes her as the heathen goddess, and softens her into woman. There is a slight degree of alarm, too, in her face; not that she really thinks anybody is looking at her, yet the idea has flitted through her mind and startled her a little. Her face is so beautiful and intellectual, that it is not dazzled out of sight by her body. Methinks this was a triumph for the sculptor to achieve. I may as well stop here. It is of no use to throw heaps of words upon her; for they all fall away, and leave her standing in chaste and naked grace, as untouched as when I began.
   I am glad to have seen this Venus, and to have found her so tender and so chaste. On the wall of the room, and to be taken in at the same glance, is a painted Venus by Titian, reclining on a couch, naked and lustful.
   The Venus de Medici has a dimple in her chin.

Nathaniel Hawthorne (1804-1864)

146

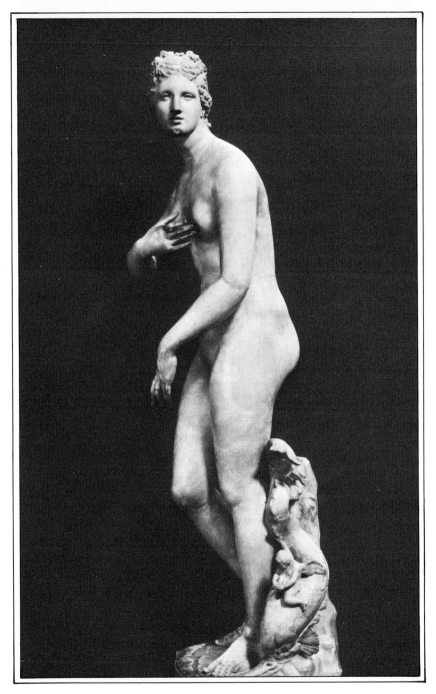

Cleomene son of Appollodoro, The Venus de Medici Uffizi Gallery (Photo Alinari)

'I cannot help thinking that there is no beauty in the features of Venus; and that the attitude is awkward and out of character. It is a bad plea to urge, that the ancients and we differ in the ideas of beauty. We know the contrary from their medals, busts, and historians.

...I was most charmed with the Venus by Titian, which has a sweetness of expression and tenderness of colouring not to be described."

Tobias Smollett (1721-1771)

TITIAN'S VENUS

You enter the Uffizi and proceed to that most-visited little gallery that exists in the world – the Tribune – and there, against the wall, without obstructing rag or leaf, you may look your fill upon the foulest, the vilest, the obscenest picture the world possesses – Titian's Venus. It isn't that she is naked and stretched out on a bed; no, it is the attitude of one of her arms and hand. If I ventured to describe the attitude, there would be a fine howl; but there the Venus lies, for anybody to gloat over that wants to; and there she has a right to lie, for she is a work of art, and Art has its privileges. I saw young girls stealing furtive glances at her; I saw young men gaze long and absorbedly at her; I saw aged, infirm men hang upon her charms with a pathetic interest. How I should like to describe her – just to see what a holy indignation I could stir up in the world – just to hear the unreflecting average man deliver himself about my grossness and coarseness, and all that. The world says that no worded description of a moving spectacle is a hundredth part as moving as the same spectacle seen with one's own eyes; yet the world is willing to let its son and its daughter and itself look at Titian's beast, but won't stand a description of it in words. Which shows that the world is not as consistent as it might be.

Mark Twain (1835-1910)

ILARIA DEL CARRETTO IN LUCCA

As he stood beside the tomb, which was wrapped in a slumbrous gleam, he asked himself, the last of many times, in what the genius of this figure consisted. As a work of the chisel, it had no claim to

Jacopo della Quercia (1374-1438), Lucca Cathedral - Tomb of Illaria del Carretto
Lucca Cathedral (Photo Alinari)

supremacy, nor was a giant's mind to be apprehended in it; yet none could approach it without a sense of personal discovery, necessary and ordained. To each newcomer, Ilaria appeared to have been awaiting him; and he bore with him afterwards a remembrance, not of having admired this among other works of art, but of private communication, as though, while he stood gazing, her silence had whispered in his ear. Jacopo della Quercia, Sparkenbroke reflected, had created here a quality that transcended his design, even his capacity – the same quality that distinguished poetry from verse, love from desire, and death itself from the physical act of dying; a quality not of the mind, for thought was an interpretation not an origin, but of the seed that falls upon certain minds gifted to receive it. The figure of this girl was neither alive with the life of the body nor dead with the death of the body, but held in the breathless quiet of one who, having seen reality through blinded eyes and touched it beyond the senses, had the genius to wait in the singleness of her expectation; and he watched the light grow upon her pillow, marvelling at her constancy, which seemed to pity and absolve him.

Charles Morgan (1894-1958)

MICHELANGELO'S NIGHT & DAY IN THE MEDICI CHAPEL

What word will God say; Michel's Night and
    Day
And Dawn and Twilight wait in marble
    scorn
    Like dogs upon a dunghill, couched on
    clay
From whence the Medicean stamp's outworn,
    The final putting off of all such sway
By all such hands, and freeing of the unborn
    In Florence and the great world outside
    Florence.
Three hundred years his patient statues wait
    In that small chapel of the dim Saint
    Lawrence:
Day's eyes are breaking bold and passionate
    Over his shoulder, and will flash abhorrence
On darkness and with level looks meet fate,

150

Michelangelo (1475- 1564), Basilica di San Lorenzo, New Sacristy,
Monument to Lorenzo de Medici Basilica de San Lorenzo (Photo Alinari)

When once loose from that marble film of
     theirs;
The Night has wild dreams in her sleep, the
     Dawn
Is haggard as the sleepless, Twilight wears
A sort of horror; as the veil withdrawn
     'Twixt the artist's soul and works had left
     them heirs
Of speechless thoughts which would not quail
     nor fawn,
     Of angers and contempts, of hope and
     love:
For not without a meaning did he place
     The princely Urbino on the seat above
With everlasting shadow on his face,
     While the slow dawns and twilights disap-
     prove
The ashes of his long-extinguished race.

Elizabeth Barrett Browning (1806-1861)

Caro m' è 'l sonno, e più l'esser di sasso,
mentre che'l danno e la vergogna dura:
non veder, non sentir, m' è gran ventura;
però non mi destar, deh! parla basso.

Slumber is sweet, but it were sweeter still
To turn to stone while shame and sorrow last,
Nor see, nor hear, and so be freed from ill;
Ah, wake me not! Whisper as you go past!

Michelangelo (1475-1564)
Translated by J. Addington Symonds (1878)

BUILDING THE DOME

   After a considerable time the architects arrived from their various
parts of the world, summoned long distances by orders given to
Florentine merchants, living in France, Germany, England and Spain,

who were told to spare no expense in securing from the rulers of those countries the services of the most skilled and intelligent artists and sending them to Florence. When the year 1420 arrived there were at last assembled in Florence all those experts from north of the Alps and from Tuscany, along with all the most able Florentine designers; and Filippo himself returned from Rome. They assembled in the Office of Works of Santa Maria del Fiore, in the presence of the wardens and consuls and a number of the most able citizens, all of whom were to listen to each artist's suggestions and then reach a decision on how to vault the cupola. So they were all called into the audience and everyone spoke his mind in turn, each architect explaining his own plan. It was wonderful to hear their strange and diverse opinions on the subject: some said that piers should be constructed from ground-level and that the arches should turn on these and support the wooden bridges for sustaining the weight; others said it would be as well to make the cupola out of pumicestone so that it would be less heavy; many others agreed that there should be a central pier and that the cupola should be raised in the form of a groined vault, like that of San Giovanni at Florence. And there were even some who suggested that the best method would be to fill it with a mixture of earth and coins so that when it was raised those who wanted to could be given permission to help themselves to the earth, and in that way they would quickly remove it all without expense. Filippo alone said that it could be raised without a great deal of woodwork, without piers or earth, at far less expense than arches would entail, and very easily without framework.

To the consuls, who had been expecting to hear him expound some beautiful scheme, and to the wardens and all the citizens present, it seemed that Filippo was talking nonsense. They mocked and laughed at him and turned away saying that he should talk about something else, and that his ideas were as mad as he was. Filippo took offence at this and said: 'Sirs, I assure you that it is impossible to raise it in any other way. You may well laugh at me, but you must understand, unless you are obstinate, that it neither should nor could be done otherwise. What is necessary, if the method I have devised is to be used, is that the cupola should be turned with the curve of appointed arch and made double, with one vault inside and the other outside so that a man can walk upright between them. And over the corners of the angles of the eight sides the fabric must be bound together through its thickness by dovetailing the stones, and likewise the sides must be bound with oaken ties. Attention must be paid to the lights, the stairways, and the conduits to draw off the rain-water. And none of you has remembered that it will be necessary to provide for internal scaffolding for the mosaics, and for countless other difficult things. But I can already envisage the completed vaulting and I know there is no method or way of doing it other than as I'm explaining.'

Filippo grew more and more heated as he was talking, and the more he tried to explain his concept so that they might understand and accept it the more sceptical their doubts about his proposal made them, until they dismissed him as an ass and a babbler. Several times he was told to leave, but he absolutely refused to go, and then he was carried out bodily by the ushers, leaving all the people at the audience convinced that he was deranged. This ignominious affair was the reason why Filippo had later to admit that he dared not walk anywhere in the city for fear of hearing people call out: 'There goes the madman.'

Giorgio Vasari (1511-1574)
Translated by G. Bull (1965)

It is somewhere mentioned that Michelangelo, when he set out from Florence to build the dome of St.Peter's, turned his horse round in the road to contemplate once more the cathedral, as he rode in the grey morning from the pines and cypresses of the city, and that he said after a pause, 'come te non voglio, meglio di te non posso.' (Like thee I will not, better than thee I cannot.)

Samuel Rogers (1763-1855)

IN SANTA CROCE WITHOUT A BAEDEKER

Tears of indignation came to Lucy's eyes, partly because Miss Lavish had jilted her, partly because she had taken her Baedeker. How could she find her way home? How could she find her way in Santa Croce? Her first morning was ruined, and she might never be in Florence again. A few minutes ago she had been all high spirits, talking as a woman of culture, and half-persuading herself that she was full of originality. Now she entered the church depressed and humiliated, not even able to remember whether it was built by the Franciscans or the Dominicans.

Of course, it must be a wonderful building. But how like a barn! And how very cold! Of course, it contained frescoes by Giotto, in the presence of whose tactile value she was capable of feeling what was proper. But who was to tell her which they were? She walked about disdainfully, unwilling to be enthusiastic over monuments of uncertain authorship or date. There was no one even to tell her which, of all the sepulchral slabs that paved the nave and transepts, was the one that was really beautiful, the one that had been most praised by Mr Ruskin.

Then the pernicious charm of Italy worked on her, and instead of acquiring information, she began to be happy. She puzzled out the Italian notices – the notice that forbade people to introduce dogs into the church – the notice that prayed people, in the interests of health and out of respect to the sacred edifice in which they found themselves not to spit. She watched the tourists: their noses were as red as their Baedekers, so cold was Santa Croce. She beheld the horrible fate that overtook three Papists – two he-babies and a she-baby - who began their career by sousing each other with the Holy Water, and then proceeded to the Machiavelli memorial, dripping, but hallowed. Advancing towards it very slowly and from immense distances, they touched the stone with their fingers, with their handkerchiefs, with their heads, and then retreated. What could this mean? They did it again and again. Then Lucy realized that they had mistaken Machiavelli for some saint, and by continual contact with his shrine were hoping to acquire virtue. Punishment followed quickly. The smallest he-baby stumbled over one of the sepulchral slabs so much admired by Mr Ruskin, and entangled his feet in the features of a recumbent bishop. Protestant as she was Lucy darted forward. She was too late. He fell heavily upon the prelate's upturned toes.

E.M. Forster (1879-1970)

PIENZA

Aeneas Silvius Piccolomini became Pope Pius II in 1458. He appointed Bernardo Rossellino, the architect, to make Pienza, his birthplace, one of the most beautiful towns in Italy.

The Pope had received many insinuations against the architect: that he had cheated; that he had blundered in the construction; that he had spent more than 50,000 ducats when his estimate had been 18,000. The law of Ephesians, according to Vitruvius, would have obliged him to make up the difference. He was a Florentine named Bernardo, hateful to the Sienese from his mere nationality. In his absence everyone abused him. Pius, when he had inspected the work and examined everything, sent for the man. When he arrived after a few days in some apprehension, since he knew that many charges had been brought against him, Pius said, 'You did well, Bernardo, in lying to us about the expense involved in the work. If you had told the truth you could never have induced us to spend so much money and neither this splendid palace nor this church, the finest in all Italy, would now be standing. Your deceit has built these glorious structures which are praised by all except the few who are consumed with envy. We thank you and think you deserve especial honour among all the architects of our time' – and he ordered full pay to be given him and in addition a present of 100 ducats and a scarlet robe. He bestowed on his son the grace he asked and charged him with new commissions. Bernardo when he heard the Pope's words, burst into tears of joy.

Pius II (1405-1464) Translated by F.A. Gragg (1960)

To The Etruscan Poets

Dream fluently, still brothers, who when young
Took with your mother's milk the mother tongue,

In which pure matrix, joining world and mind,
You strove to leave some line of verse behind

Like a fresh track across a field of snow,
Not reckoning that all could melt and go.

Richard Wilbur (1921-)

Tuscan Language

The Tuscan language is renowned throughout Italy for its purity.

As for the language of Florence, it's pure, but in their books, not in their throats: they do so choak it in the throat that it's almost quite drowned there. Nor doth it recover itself again till it come to Rome, where *Lingua Toscana in bocca Romana* is a most sweet language.

R. Lassels (1603?-1668)

COUNT RUCELLAI – An Obituary

His Tuscan patriotism sometimes came out in surprising ways. Motoring in Florence some years ago he was held up by road works and heard one of the road menders swearing. Getting out of his car he went up to the man and said to him. 'Sir, we are Tuscans, so have to set an example of good speech. That is our duty, so we shouldn't use swear words however cross we may feel or however provoking the circumstances.' This was said in so serious yet friendly a tone that the road mender apologized, thanked him and promised to try to remember his duty better in future.

John Bury (The Times 1983)

Some other reasons for the richness and variety of the Italian language are the following:

(1) That we have never given up any of our riches, however old...

(2) The great liveliness, imagination, fecundity, and variety of the gifts of our writers, qualities which appertain to a nation which has adapted itself to all sorts of circumstances, enterprises, characters, and purposes.

(3) The large extent to which our written language (for it is of this that we are speaking, and comparing with foreign languages) is indebted to the spoken speech of the people...

A nation, especially as lively a one as the Italian, and in particular the Tuscan, and very civilized besides (as the Tuscans and Italians were before any other people in Europe), and constantly in touch with other peoples (as indeed Tuscany has been, both owing to her reputation for culture, her political circumstances, her freedom, and especially her trade), naturally invents or adopts a very large number of words and idioms and many forms of both. These, however, unless the use and form of them is spread by the written word (which varies all over the country), to establish their form and meaning and ensure their permanence, will not spread very far nor become very precise, but will remain uncertain, fluctuating, and arbitrary, and will soon be lost, with new ones taking their place. But Italian literature has done precisely what I have specified. It has adopted with a greater care than any other literature, and with great goodwill and delight, many popular expressions, idioms, and forms, especially the Tuscan, and has itself been formed by them...

The pseudo-philosophers may say what they please. A richness which consists of variety, beauty, expression, efficacy, force, brio, grace, ease, softness, naturalness, will never belong and never has belonged to any language that has not been drawn from the popular tongue, not only originally but constantly, and not by writing as the people speak, but by turning what has been adopted from the people into the universal forms and rules of literature and of the national language.

Giacomo Leopardi (1798-1837) Translated by Iris Origo (1902-)

A Night At The Opera

English travellers have not always found the opera in Italy quite to their taste.

There is a tolerable opera in Florence for the entertainment of the best company, though they do not seem very attentive to the music. Italy is certainly the native country of this art; and yet I do not find the people in general, either more musically inclined, or better provided with ears than their neighbours.

Tobias Smollett (1721-1771)

He had been to this theatre many years before, on the occasion of a performance of *La Zia di Carlo*. Since then it had been thoroughly done up, in the tints of the beetroot and the tomato, and was in many other ways a credit to the little town. The orchestra had been enlarged, some of the boxes had terracotta draperies, and over each box was now suspended an enormous tablet, neatly framed, bearing upon it the number of that box. There was also a drop-scene, representing a pink and purple landscape, wherein sported many a lady lightly clad, and two more ladies lay along the top of the proscenium to steady a large and pallid clock. So rich and so appalling was the effect that Philip could scarcely suppress a cry. There is something majestic in the bad taste of Italy; it is not the bad taste of a country which knows no better; it has not the nervous vulgarity of England, or the blinded vulgarity of Germany. It observes beauty, and chooses to pass it by. But it attains to beauty's confidence. This tiny theatre of Monteriano spraddled and swaggered with the best of them, and these ladies with their clock would have nodded to the young men on the ceiling of the Sistine.

Philip had tried for a box, but all the best were taken; it was rather a grand performance, and he had to be content with stalls. Harriet was fretful and insular. Miss Abbott was pleasant, and insisted on praising everything; her only regret was that she had no pretty clothes with her.

'We do all right,' said Philip, amused at her unwonted vanity.

'Yes, I know; but pretty things pack as easily as ugly ones. We had no need to come to Italy like guys.'

This time he did not reply, 'But we're here to rescue a baby.' For he saw a charming picture, as charming a picture as he had seen for years – the hot red theatre; outside the theatre, towers and dark gates and medieval walls; beyond the walls, olive-trees in the starlight and white winding roads and fireflies and untroubled dust; and here in the middle of it all Miss Abbott, wishing she had not come looking like a guy. She had made the right remark. Most undoubtedly she had made the right remark. This still suburban woman was unbending before the shrine.

'Don't you like it all?' he asked her.

'Most awfully.' And by this bald interchange they convinced each other that Romance was here.

Harriet, meanwhile, had been coughing ominously at the drop-scene, which presently rose on the grounds of Ravenswood, and the chorus of Scotch retainers burst into cry. The audience accompanied with tappings and drummings, swaying in the melody like corn in the wind. Harriet, though she did not care for music, knew how to listen to it. She uttered an acid 'Shish!'

'Shut it,' whispered her brother.

'We must make a stand from the beginning. They're talking.'

'It is tiresome,' murmured Miss Abbott; 'but perhaps it isn't for us to interfere.'

Harriet shook her head and shished again. The people were quiet not because it is wrong to talk during a chorus, but because it is natural to be civil to a visitor. For a little time she kept the whole house in order, and could smile at her brother complacently.

Her success annoyed him. He had grasped the principle of opera in Italy – it aims not at illusion but at entertainment – and he did not want this great evening party to turn into a prayer-meeting. But soon the boxes began to fill, and Harriet's power was over. Families greeted each other across the auditorium. People in the pit hailed their brothers and sons in the chorus, and told them how well they were singing. When Lucia appeared by the fountain there was loud applause, and cries of 'Welcome to Monteriano!'

'Ridiculous babies!' said Harriet, settling down in her stall.

'Why, it is the famous hot lady of the Apennines,' cried Philip; 'the one who had never, never before –'

'Ugh! Don't. She will be very vulgar. And I'm sure it's even worse here than in the tunnel. I wish we'd never – '

Lucia began to sing, and there was a moment's silence. She was stout and ugly; but her voice was still beautiful, and as she sang the theatre murmured like a hive of happy bees. All through the coloratura she was accompanied by sighs, and its top note was drowned in a shout of universal joy.

So the opera proceeded. The singers drew inspiration from the audience, and the two great sextets were rendered not unworthily. Miss Abbott fell into the spirit of the thing. She, too, chatted and laughed and applauded and encored, and rejoiced in the existence of beauty. As for Philip, he forgot himself as well as his mission. He was not even an enthusiastic visitor. For he had been in this place always. It was his home.

Harriet, like M. Bovary on a more famous occasion, was trying to follow the plot. Occasionally she nudged her companions, and asked them what had become of Walter Scott. She looked around grimly. The audience sounded drunk, and even Caroline, who never took a drop, was swaying oddly. Violent waves of excitement, all arising from very little, went sweeping round the theatre. The climax was reached in the mad scene. Lucia, clad in white, as befitted her malady, suddenly gathered up her streaming hair and bowed her acknowledgments to the audience. Then from the back of the stage – she feigned not to see it – there advanced a kind of bamboo clothes-horse, stuck all over with bouquets. It was very ugly, and most of the flowers in it were false.

Lucia knew this, and so did the audience; and they all knew that the clothes-horse was a piece of stage property, brought in to make the performance go year after year. None the less did it unloose the great deeps. With a scream of amazement and joy she embraced the animal, pulled out one or two practicable blossoms, pressed them to her lips and flung them into her admirers. They flung them back, with loud melodious cries, and a little boy in one of the stage-boxes, snatched up his sister's carnations and offered them. 'Che carino!' exclaimed the singer. She darted at the little boy and kissed him. Now the noise became tremendous. 'Silence! Silence!' shouted many old gentlemen behind. 'Let the divine creature continue!' But the young men in the adjacent box were imploring Lucia to extend her civility to them. She refused, with a humorous expressive gesture. One of them hurled a bouquet at her. She spurned it with her foot. Then, encouraged by the roars of the audience, she picked it up and tossed it to them. Harriet was always unfortunate. The bouquet struck her full in the chest, and a little *billet-doux* fell out of it into her lap. 'Call this classical,' she cried, rising from her seat. 'It's not even respectable! Philip! Take me out at once.'

E.M. Forster (1879-1970)

DANTE

Even after his death he did not return
to the city that nursed him
Going away this man did not look back.
To him I sing this song.
Torches, night, a last embrace,
outside in her streets the mob howling.
He sent her a curse from hell
and in heaven could not forget her.
But never, in a penitent's shirt,
did he walk barefoot with lighted candle
through his beloved Florence,
perfidious, base and irremediably home.

Anna Akhmatova (1889-1966)
Translated by S. Kunitz & M. Hayward (1967).

Anonymous Sketch (Siena: mid 16th century) Victoria and Albert Museum Crown ©

CHAPTER 8

EVERYDAY LIFE

Cerchi chi vuol le pompe e gli altri
  onori,
Le piazze, i tempii e gli edifizi magni
Le delizie, il tesor, quale accompagni
Mille duri pensier, mille dolori.
Un verde praticel pien di bei fiori,
Un rivolo che l'erba intorno bagni
Un augelletto che d'amor si lagni
Acqueta molto meglio i nostri ardori;
L'ombrose selve, i sassi e gli alti monti
Gli antri oscuri, e le fere fuggitive,
Qualche leggiadra ninfa paurosa,
Quivi vegg'io con pensier vaghi e pronti
Le belle luci come fosser vive;
Qui me le toglie or una or altra cosa.

'Let him who will seek pomp and honours, public squares, temples
and great buildings, pleasures and rewards which bring with them a
thousand distracting thoughts, a thousand troubles. A green meadow
full of lovely flowers, a stream which washes the grass on its banks, a
little bird that makes it plaint of love, these soothe our restlessness far
better. There the leafy woods, the rocks, the high hills, the dark caves,
the wild animals in flight and some graceful timid nymph quickly
bring before my mind my love's bright eyes as if they were alive before
me. Here (i.e. in the city) one thing after another robs me of them.'

Lorenzo de Medici (1449-1492)
Translated by C. M. Ady (1955)

UP AT A VILLA – DOWN IN THE CITY

(As Distinguished by an Italian Person of Quality).

I

Had I but plenty of money, money
  enough and to spare
The house for me, no doubt were a house
  in the city-square;
Ah, such a life, such a life, as one leads at
  the window there!

Fra Angelico (1387-1455), The Deposition (detail) San Marco Florence (Photo Alinari)

Something to see, by Bacchus, something
  to hear, at least!
There, the whole day long, one's life is a
  perfect feast;
While up at a villa one lives, I maintain it,
  no more than a beast.

III

Well now, look at our villa! stuck like the
  horn of a bull
Just on a mountain's edge as bare as the
  creature's skull,
Save a mere shag of a bush with hardly a
  leaf to pull!
– I scratch my own, sometimes, to see if
  the hair's turned wool.

IV

But the city, oh the city – the square with
  the houses! Why?
They are stone-faced, white as a curd,
  there's something to take the eye!
Houses in four straight lines, not a single
  front awry!
You watch who crosses and gossips, who
  saunters, who hurries by;
Green blinds, as a matter of course, to
  draw when the sun gets high;
And the shops with fanciful signs which
  are painted properly.

V

What of a villa? Though winter be over in
  March by rights,
'Tis May perhaps ere the snow shall have
  withered well off the heights:
You've the brown ploughed land before,
  where the oxen steam and wheeze,
And the hills over-smoked behind by the
  faint grey olive-trees.

Is it better in May, I ask you? you've
  summer all at once;
In a day he leaps complete with a few
  strong April suns!
'Mid the sharp short emerald wheat,
  scarce risen three fingers well,
The wild tulip, at end of its tube, blows
  out its great red bell
Like a thin clear bubble of blood, for the
  children to pick and sell.

Robert Browning (1812-89)

To Guido Machiavelli, In Florence

Guido, my darling boy, I have had a letter from you which has given
me the greatest pleasure, especially because you say you are quite well
again; I could not have had better news. For as long as God grants you
– and me – life, I think if you are prepared to play your part I shall give
you a good start in life, for besides the influential friends I already have,
I have become friendly with Cardinal Cibo, so much so that I am
surprised at it myself, and this will stand you in good stead. But you
must study, and now you can no longer plead sickness, work really
hard at your books and at music; you see what honour my own little
learning brings to me. So, my child, if you want to please me, and to
bring profit and credit to yourself, work with a will, for everyone will
help you if you help yourself.

Since the little mule has lost its wits it must be treated quite the
contrary to other madmen: for other madmen are bound fast, and I
want you to let this one go. Give him to Vangelo and tell him to take
him to Montepugliano and then take off his halter and bridle and let
him go where he wants to make his own way and work off his madness.
The countryside is large, the beast is small, he can do no harm; and so
we can watch what happens without any trouble, and if he recovers his
senses it will always be possible for you to catch him again. As for the
other horses, do as Lodovico told you. Thank God he has recovered,
and that he sold them – and I know this was the right thing to do; they
were too expensive to keep – but I am surprised and saddened that he
has not written.

Greet Mona Marietta and tell her that I have been on the point of leaving here day after day, and still am, and I have never longed to be in Florence so much as now; but there is nothing else I can do. Simply say that whatever she hears she must be sure I will be there before any trouble arrives. Give Baccina a kiss, and Piero, and Totto if he is there: I would dearly like to know if his eyes are better. Be happy, and spend as little as you can. And remind Bernardo to behave himself – I have written to him twice in the last fortnight and have had no reply. Christ keep you all.

Niccolò Machiavelli (1469-1527)
Translated by J.R. Hale (1961)

FOUR SONGS OF THE ITALIAN EARTH:

OLD PEPPINO, THE PEASANT

(1) *Spring Morning*

Not so fine,
But warm, oh, warm
With an early smell of straw, of orris and roses.

Listening clouds of sleep
Hang upon towers
As roses cling to walls,
Press the glistening flowers
Into the warm, damp earth again.

The little pigs squeal among the trodden straw,
The strawberries are sodden.
Under the eaves in the sweet, invisible rain
The birds chirp and gurgle in the gutters.

'Is it fog that nuzzles my hand?'
The old man mutters,
'Damp and white is the fur of the old hunting-dog,
White and damp as fog,
His coat smells of wet, but also of days that were good,
When I was not stiff as wood in each bone
And we both slept less in the sun of an afternoon.'

169

(2) *Summer*

Sun dissolves to re-create.
Brick smoulders
Plaster moulders in the sun.
In the sun.

On the riven ground
The sweat of my labour falls all day like the rain.
Each night I die,
And in the morn am born again.
No time for my gun!
Yet I wipe my hair back from my forehead,
Look round me.
Not a bird in sight!
Flowers blow: mountains show:
Fruit and sky grow and glow.

What is the day's beat,
In the summer's husk?
Men calling in the fields,
Wheels creaking through the buzz and hum of summer.
But at night, in the heart of the heat.
The sounds are different,
Whether dry or glutinous:
The rhythmical, high shuffle of the cicada among the grass
The cool, cold-blooded cry of hunting owls
Who float and flap luminously in the darkness,
And over all, the primal chant of earth, that of
The frogs, within their thick and mottled skins,
Croaking their common sense, croaking
In patches of warm wet darkness,
Lost in the universe;
Voices that only die when,
After the day's first burst of tumbling, grumbling bells,
The chant of the priests begins.

(3) *Autumn*

The moth hums under the beams
In the shuttered rooms,
Cool in their darkness, enclosed in autumn's glow
As the stone of the peach is bitter within sweet flesh.

The moth hums and hovers under the rafters.
And below, men sing as they swing the oar of the wine
Till the sharp juice spurts on the pavement and dyes it
And the acrid scent sours the air,
Crisp and blue with the smoke of bonfires.

Now my dog whines to be out,
And we go with my gun,
Walking stiffly into the light of the evening, the light
    mountains,
Into the very eye of the sun,
Until as I hide, to aim,
The cypress and I grow one.

(4) *Winter*

Rime lies crisp upon the ground,
But not in the great marshes.
There, the angry snout of the boar
Brushes aside the rushes.

In villages, tilted upon hills,
The swarthy, innocent-faced shepherds
Squeal on their wooden trumpets,
Squeak on their bagpipes;
Before the gold-haloed Virgin.

On the hills, under flat-topped pines,
The flames that were lit by the resting huntsmen
Die like stars in a moment's sunshine
And leave a glistening ring upon the earth.

Osbert Sitwell (1892-1969)

FRIENDSHIP

The merchant Francesco Datini showed his friendship for Ser Lapo Mazzei by showering him with gifts of food and drink.

Although a poor man, Ser Lapo did not feel any false pride about accepting such favours. 'I use you and your possessions', he told Francesco, 'as if they were my own', for he held that 'a man who does not make a friend's wishes his own, is neither courteous nor a friend'. Nor did he object to jogging Francesco's memory, when necessary, as is shown by the following charming request in September 1392, for some of the new oil from Il Palco:

If you were like me, you would say 'Ser Lapo, I have some good oil, and perhaps yours is not so sweet...' And you would say, 'It is in such and such a place, and I have ordered it to be given to you.'... And I would use it, as if it were my own. For I do not consider myself a paid labourer, but a servant of love.

But when Francesco, with the lavish ostentatiousness which alternated with his stinginess, sent far too much of the requested gift, Ser Lapo's pride and taste were both offended. 'Do not believe that sweet oil, bestowed by a friend, does not please me. But, in faith, too much of it gives me no pleasure.'

But Francesco could not learn. Once he sent Ser Lapo so big a load of cheese that his friend wrote, 'I deem myself a notary turned cheese-monger', and, twenty years later, he was still protesting:

'The peasant who asked God to give him a little water for his millet was not pleased when a flood came into his house. And neither was I, when, having asked for a couple of melons, I received a whole load, and enough wine for a month.'

Iris Origo (1902-)

A Breef Rehersall Of The Chiefe Conditions And Qualities In A Courtier

Castiglione resided at the Court of Urbino where he laid out his qualifications for the complete man in his widely influential book 'Il Cortegiano' (1528)

To be well borne and of good stocke.
To be of meane stature, rather with the least then to high, and well made to his proportion.
Not to be womanish in his sayings or doings.
To play for his pastime at Dice and Cardes, not wholye for moneis sake, nor fume and chafe in his losse.
To speake and write the language that is most in use emonge the

172

the commune people, without inventing new woordes, inckhorn
tearmes or straunge phases, and such as be growen out
of use by long time.

To gete him an especiall and hartye friend to companye

To speake alwaies of matters likely, least he be counted a lyer in
reporting of wonders and straunge miracles.

To daunce well without over nimble footinges or to busie trickes.

> To swimme well.
> To leape well.
> To renn well.
> To vaute well.
> To wrastle well.
> To cast the stone well.
> To cast the barr well.

> Sildome in open sight of the people
> but privilye with himselfe alone, or
> emonge hys friendes and familiers.

> To renn well at tilt, and at ring.
> To tourney.
> To fight at Barriers.
> To kepe a passage or streict.
> To play at Jogo di Canne.
> To renn at Bull.
> To fling a Speare or Dart.

> These things in open syght to delyte
> the commune people withall.

Not to renn, wrastle, leape, nor cast the stone or barr with men of the
Countrey, except he be sure to gete the victorie.

To undertake his bould feates and couragious enterprises in warr, out
of companye and in the sight of the most noble personages in the
campe, and (if it be possible) beefore his Princis eyes.

Not to love promotions so, that a man shoulde thinke he coulde not
live without them, nor unshamefastlye to begg any office.

To refuse them after such a comelye sort, that the Prince offrynge hym
them, maye have a cause to offre them with a more instance.

Not to presse to his Prince where ever he be, to hould him with a vaine

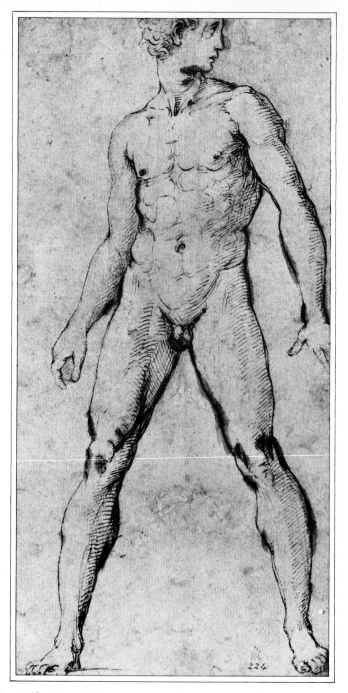

?copy of a lost Raphael (1483-1520) Victoria and Albert Museum Crown ©

tale, that others should thinke him in favour with him.
His conversation with women to be alwayes gentle, sober, meeke, lowlie, modest, serviceable, comelie, merie, not bitinge or sclaundering with jeste, nippes, frumpes, or railinges, the honesty of any.

Baldssare Castiglione (1478-1529)
Translated by T. Hoby (1552/3 pub. 1561)

In the 1390's Datini the Merchant sent Household Instructions to his young wife frequently

Remember to go to bed betimes and rise early and let not the door be opened until you have got up. And look well to everything; let them not go a-gadding. You know what Bartolomea is: she will say she goes to one place, and then goes elsewhere. Ghirigora, too, has little sense; do not let her be without you. There is greater need of vigilance than when I am there... Now behave in such a way that I need not scold. You cannot err in watching over them well, and it will come easily to you... Now strive to be a woman and no longer a child; soon you will be entering your twenty-fifth year.

Francesco Datini (14th-15th centuries) Translated by Iris Origo (1902-)

MARCH: now come violent winds which blow away the oak leaves at last, and for a short time the country is at its most naked. It seems a sort of ritual purge and cleansing before the spring explodes.

Now it is hot when the sun shines, and on these days the first snakes emerge from hibernation. They are very sleepy and will lie coiled in neat and perfect circles in the sun. Even the vipers look rather appealing as they doze so defencelessly. Some of the harmless snakes are quite large – well over three feet and thick in proportion – with beautiful black and yellow markings which look greenish as they slip through the thick undergrowth that they love; they are gentle, timid and amiable creatures. Now too the lizards are appearing.

The early spring flowers are out in profusion; violets, primroses, wild daffodils, periwinkle, wood anenomes. There is peach, apricot, sloe blossom everywhere.

The garden is full of finches and tits all busy nest-building – every year the Italian sparrows and the tits nest in their same holes in the crumbling old stone walls of the house.

175

Another sign of approaching Easter – here is the *parroco* with incense
and a retinue of small boys to give the house its annual blessing.

Raymond Flower (pub. 1978)

A TUSCAN LULLABY

Maria lavava,
Giuseppe stendeva,
Suo Figlio piangeva
Dal Freddo che aveva.
 – Sta zitto, mio figlio,
Chè adesso ti piglio!
Del latte t' ho dato,
Del pane 'un ce n' è.–
 La neve sui monti
Cadeva dal cielo:
Maria col suo velo
Copriva Gesù.

Sweet Mary was washing,
While Joseph laid, drying,
The Baby was crying
For the cold that came on.
 Oh hush thee, my darling,
I'll take thee this moment,–
Of milk I have given thee,
Of bread there is none.
 The snow on the mountains
From heaven was falling:
Then Mary her veil took
and covered her Son.

Roadside Song

To His Daughter

Contessina was Lorenzo's favourite daughter.

My Contessina. – I hear that you ask about me every hour, how I am, and when I shall return, so I write to you that, by the grace of God, I am very well, and hope, if it pleases God, to return as well as ever I was. I shall come back soon, and in a few days I shall be there to see you. Take care that I find you well and cheerful, so pray to God for me, and caress Alfonsina, and tell her from me to make much of the baby. I hear that Monsignore and the other children went away early. They did not do well to leave you all alone but I shall soon be back, and they can stay in the country by themselves. Salute your Piro and Niccolò and all the others from me when you see them.

Lorenzo De Medici (1449-1492)
Translated by Y. Maguire (1936)

A Letter

I live, then, on my farm, and have not spent twenty days in all in Florence since my late adventures. Up till recently I have been snaring thrushes with my own hands. I used to get up before daybreak, prepared the birdlime and went out with such a bundle of cages on my back that I looked like Geta when he came back from the port with Amphitrion's books. I would catch at least two, at the most six, thrushes. And so I passed the whole of September; since then this recreation has come to an end – and I regret it, odd and trivial as it was.

I will tell you what my life is now. I get up in the morning with the sun, and go into a wood of mine I am having cut down. I spend an hour or two there looking over the work done on the previous day and passing the time with the woodcutters, who always have some quarrel on their hands, among themselves or with their neighbours. As to this wood, I could tell you a thousand good stories about my dealings with Frosino da Panzano and others who want firewood from it. Frosino in particular sent for certain piles of wood without a word to me, and when he came to pay he wanted to keep back ten lire which he said he had won off me four years before when he beat me at *cricca* at Antonio Guicciardini's. I began to raise the devil and was on the point of charging the carter who had fetched it with theft, when Giovanni Machiavelli stepped in and made peace. When we had that spell of cold weather, Batista Guicciardini, Filippo Ginori, Tommaso del Bene and some other citizens all undertook to buy a load from me. I gave my word to them all, and sent one to Tommaso which only looked like half a load when it arrived in Florence, because he and his wife, his children and the servants were all there to stack it; it was like Gabburra and his lads butchering an ox on a Thursday. So when I saw who was getting the profit, I told the others that I had no wood left; and they have all taken it badly, especially Batista, who adds this to the other woes that followed the sack of Prato.

When I leave the wood I go to a spring and on from there with a book under my arm, Dante or Petrarch, or one of the minor poets, Tibullus, Ovid or someone like that to an *uccellare* which I have. I read of their amorous passions and their loves; I remember my own – and for a while these reflections make me happy. Then I move on along the road, to the inn, talking to passers-by, asking news of the places they come from, hearing about this and that, and observing the various tastes and fancies of mankind. This brings me to lunch time, when I and my brood eat such food as this poor farm and my slender patrimony provides. When I have eaten, I go back to the inn, where I usually find the landlord, a butcher, a miller and a couple of bakers. With these I act the rustic for the rest of the day, playing at *cricca* and *tric-trac,* which lead to a thousand squabbles and countless slanging-matches – our fights are usually over a farthing but we can be heard shouting none the less from San Casciano. So, trapped among this vermin I rub the mould from my wits and work off the sense of being so cruelly treated by Fate – content to be driven on along this road if only to watch for her to show some sign of shame.

When evening comes, I return home and go into my study. On the threshold I strip off my muddy, sweaty, workday clothes and put on the robes of court and palace, and in this graver dress I enter the antique courts of the ancients and am welcomed by them, and there I taste the food that alone is mine, and for which I was born. And there I make bold to speak to them and ask the motives of their actions, and they, in their humanity, reply to me. And for the space of four hours I forget the world, remember no vexation, fear poverty no more, tremble no more at death: I pass indeed into their world. And as Dante says that there can be no understanding without the memory retaining what it has heard, I have written down what I have gained from their conversation, and composed a small work *De principatibus,* where I dive as deep as I can into ideas about this subject, discussing the nature of princely rule, what forms it takes, how these are acquired, how they are maintained, why they are lost. And if you have ever been pleased by any of my fancies, this should not displease you. And it should be acceptable to a prince, and especially to a new prince. So I am dedicating it to his Magnificence, Giuliano. Filippo Casavecchia has seen it; he can give you details both of the work itself and the talk we have had about it, though I am constantly plumping and grooming it.

Niccolò Machiavelli (1469-1527)
Translated by J.R. Hale (1961)

BENVENUTO CELLINI CATCHES A FEVER IN FLORENCE

Signor Ulivieri happened to have occasion to go to Florence to dispose of some filings of gold and silver, and as I had in that unwholesome air caught a slight fever, I returned, whilst it was upon me, with my master to Florence; where my father secretly entreated my master, in the most urgent manner, not to carry me back again to Pisa. My fever, still continuing, I kept my bed about two months, and my father attended me with the greatest affection imaginable, telling me repeatedly that he thought it a thousand years till I recovered, that he might hear me play upon the flute; but feeling my pulse, as he had a smattering of physic and some learning, he perceived so great a change in it whenever he mentioned the flute, that he was often frightened, and left me, in tears. Observing then the great concern he was in, I bade one of my sisters, bring me a flute; for, though I had a fever constantly upon me, the instrument was a very easy one, and would do me no hurt. I thereupon played with such skill and dexterity, that my father, entering the room on a sudden, gave me a thousand blessings, assuring me that, during my absence from him, I had made great improvement. He requested, moreover, that I would endeavour to continue my progress, and not neglect so admirable a qualification.

But no sooner had I recovered my health, than I returned to my worthy friend, the goldsmith Marcone, who put me in a way of making money; and with my gains I assisted my father and my relations.

Benvenuto Cellini (1500-71)
Translated by T. Roscoe (1822)

Galileo was born in Pisa but spent much of his life in his villa in Arcetri above Florence. Among his important discoveries were the isochronism of the pendulum, Jupiter's satellites and the libration of the moon.

...From Tuscan Bellosguardo,
Where Galileo stood at nights to take
The vision of the stars, we have found it hard,
Gazing upon the earth and heavens, to make
A choice of beauty.

Elizabeth Barrett Browning (1806-61)

' ...It is true. I do go on speculating, but to the great prejudice of my health; for thinking, joined to various other molestations, destroys my sleep, and increases the melancholy of my nights; while the pleasure which I have taken hitherto in making observations on new phenomena is almost entirely gone. I have observed a most marvellous appearance on the surface of the Moon. Though she has been looked at such millions of times by such millions of men, I do not find that any have observed the slightest alteration in her surface but that exactly the same side has always been supposed to be represented to our eyes. Now I find that such is not the case, but on the contrary that she changes her aspect, as one who, having his full face turned towards us, should move it sideways, first to the right and then to the left, or should raise and then lower it, and lastly incline it first to the right and then to the left shoulder. All these changes I see in the Moon; and the large, anciently known spots which are seen in her face, may help to make evident the truth of what I say. Add to this a second marvel, which is that these three mutations have their three several periods, the first daily, the second monthly, the third yearly. Now what connexion does your Reverence think these three lunar periods may have with the daily, monthly and annual movement of the sea? which is ruled by the Moon, the consent of all.'

Galileo Galilei (1564-1642)

Gli uomini hanno gli anni chè sentono, e le donne quelli che mostrano' (Men count the years they feel and women those they show).

Popular saying

To Fuscus Salinator

Pliny's villa was just outside the Tuscan border near Civitella.

You want to know how I plan the summer days I spend in Tuscany. I wake when I like, usually about sunrise, often earlier but rarely later. My shutters stay closed, for in the stillness and darkness I feel myself surprisingly detached from any distractions and left to myself in freedom; my eyes do not determine the direction of my thinking, but, being unable to see anything, they are guided to visualise my thoughts. If I have anything on hand I work it out in my head, choosing and correcting the wording, and the amount I achieve depends on the ease or difficulty with which my thoughts can be marshalled and kept in my head. Then I call my secretary, the shutters are opened, and I dictate what I have put into shape; he goes out, is recalled, and again dismissed. Three or four hours after I first wake (but I don't keep to fixed times) I betake myself according to the weather either to the terrace or the covered arcade, work out the rest of my subject, and dictate it. I go for a drive, and spend the time in the same way as when walking or lying down; my powers of concentration do not flag and are in fact refreshed by the change. After a short sleep and another walk I read a Greek or Latin speech aloud and with emphasis, not so much for the sake of my voice as my digestion, though of course both are strengthened by this. Then I have another walk, am oiled, take exercise, and have a bath. If I am dining alone with my wife or with a few friends, a book is read aloud during the meal and afterwards we listen to a comedy or some music; then I walk again with the members of my household, some of whom are well educated. Thus the evening is prolonged with varied conversations, and even when the days are at their longest, comes to a satisfying end.

Sometimes I vary this routine, for, if I have spent a long time on my couch or taking a walk, after my siesta and reading I go out on horseback instead of in a carriage so as to be quicker and take less time. Part of the day is given up to friends who visit me from neighbouring towns and sometimes come to my aid with a welcome interruption when I am tired. Occasionally I go hunting, but not without my notebooks so that I shall have something to bring home even if I catch nothing. I also give some time to my tenants (they think it should be more) and the boorishness of their complaints gives fresh zest to our literary interests and the more civilized pursuits of town.

Pliny The Younger (b. AD6l)
Translated by B. Radice (1963)

The moralistic Fior di Virtù *was published in 1482, a turning point in Florentine history. Lorenzo's golden age was drawing to a close and Girolamo Savonarola had become prior of San Marco, demanding that the people renounce their luxurious, profligate ways.*

Of truthfulness we read in the lives of the Holy Fathers. There was a great and gracious nobleman once who had left the world and great wealth and had gone to serve God in a monastery. One day, the Abbot, thinking that this man would be more versed than others in the ways of the world, sent him to market with certain aged donkeys with the instruction to sell the beasts and then buy some younger ones. And the Abbot sent another friar, a lay brother, with him to sell the donkeys. At the market the people asked our monk whether the donkeys were good. The monk answered: 'Do you think that our monastery is so gone to seed that we would be selling the donkeys if they were any good?' And the people asked: 'Why are their tails and their backs so skinned?' The monk answered: 'Because they are old and unable to carry their loads. Often they fall under their loads and we must grab them by their tails to lift them back. And their backs are skinned by numberless thrashings.' The beasts were not sold. Back at the monastery the lay brother who had been out with the monk told the Abbot all that had happened at the market. The Abbot sent for the monk and scolded him harshly. The monk answered: 'Father, do you think that I embraced this religion to deceive others and to damn my soul telling lies to sell a few donkeys? Don't you know that I have left many donkeys and horses, houses and possessions and many other riches behind me in the world just to come and serve the one who is supreme and pure truth and to escape the lies of this false world? I always disliked lies and in this place I dislike them even more.' Hearing such words, the Abbot was unable to answer or to contradict.

from Fior di Virtù *(pub. 1482)*
Translated by N. Fersin (1953)

A LETTER

Lucrezia was the eldest daughter of Il Magnifico.

My magnificent Grandmother. Let me know how you are, and when you began your baths. It seems to me a thousand years until you return, and every day I say a Paternoster and an Ave Maria, so that you may return well and happy. Please send me the basket of things you promised me. All we children are here at Careggi with Mona Clarice and Mona Bartolomea is here with all her family. Tell Lionardo that they are all well, and commend me to him. We very often go to your fountain, and there we all talk of you. Lorenzo has gone to Pisa. May God be with him, so that he may soon return to us here. Please enjoy yourself for love of me, so that you may return joyful and happy, which seems to me a thousand years hence. If I can do anything for you, command me. No more. Christ guard you from all ill.

Lucrezia de Medici, aged 7 (b. 1470)
Translated by Y. Maguire (1936)

COMING HOME

When the olives were ripening at Christmas in the groves of Bozzano, I gecchia and Massarosa I came home; and then again at Easter when Viareggio glowed in the hot Spring sunlight and the cafés were thronged with the Englishmen who came to stand mournfully round the monument which marks the place where Shelley's body was burned along the shores of the sea; and then again in the summer when the heat-haze hung over the rice-fields and the voices of village girls working barefoot in the flooded paddies rose like bird-song in the dawn mist – I came from the Seminary of San Martino in Lucca to my home in Quiesa.

Home was a simple house crowded with five children, three girls and two boys. We played in the piazza of the church or raced to the lake where we begged our way into the fishermen's boats or wandered with the olive-pickers in the groves, and when the men swung their long bamboo poles and tapped the branches to loosen the ripe fruit, we scrambled in the grass and filled the baskets with olives.

Home was the opportunity to see my great-uncle, Don Antonio, a musician who became canon, though no one ever looked less like a church dignitary. It was not his habit to wear the Roman cassock. Instead, it pleased him to wear an eighteenth-century uniform, comprising a frock coat with black silk knee breeches, black silk stockings and black slippers ornamented with silver buckles. Dignified, but never aloof, he possessed a formidable memory for music: as an old man, he could still entertain his friends with the entire score of *Cavalleria Rusticana*. The venerable canon adored opera, and he was loud in his disappointment when Pope Pius X forbade playing anything in church which savored of the theatre. Don Antonio was heard muttering: 'As Pope I revere him, but as a musician he is unworthy.'

So while my great-uncle spoke about music the summers followed one another, with little to break the slow rhythm of those languorous days when the grapes are swelling and sweetening on the vines, and the noons are charged with the dry chatter of the cicadas, and in the hot breathless nights thousands of frogs in the rice-fields croak to the moon. And though the name of Puccini was often mentioned, and I associated the name with his Operas, I associated it still more with the roaring devil of a motor-car he owned, a car which fascinated and terrified the simple people accustomed to the slow pace of oxen and donkeys. This car tore over the unpaved roads between Torre del Lago and Viareggio, and around the lake to Quiesa and Massaciuccoli and on to Lucca, sending the peasants scuttling like rabbits, causing the pious to cross themselves devoutly as they escaped with their lives. I had never set eyes on Puccini, and more than anything else I longed to see him.

Dante del Fiorentino (pub. 1952)

LATE AUTUMN AT A TUSCAN CASTLE

(1) *By Day*

By day
   The sun is snared
In the airy cages of the fruit trees,
Revealing the gold fur along their branches,
   Throwing down golden rings
   To quiver in the water
     In grotto and fountain.

(2) *By Night*

By night
   The tower top
Becomes a chamber of the stars.

Down below the rooms are black and silent,
But the weathercock creaks in the wind from the mountains
    Matching the sound of an armoured host:
It jangles again,
    Spins round in circles
Like a witch on a broomstick.

Osbert Sitwell (1892-1969)

IMAGES AND SHADOWS

At the Villa Medici, Fiesole

Whenever I was free of my governesses, I escaped into the garden, not to the formal terrace, with its box-edged beds and fountains where my mother took her guests, but to the dark ilex wood above it or the steep terraces of the *podere,* partly cultivated with plots of wheat or of fragrant beans, partly abandoned to high grass and to the untended bushes of the tangled, half-wild little pink Tuscan roses, perpetually-flowering, *le rose d'ogni mese.* This became my own domain. The great stone blocks of the Etruscan wall were as good for climbing, with their easy footholds, as were the low-branched olive-trees; the high grass between the rose-bushes was a perfect place in which to lie hidden with a book on a summer's day, peering down, unseen, at the dwarfed figures of the grown-ups staidly conversing on the terrace far below; and the deep Etruscan well in the midst of the ilex wood, its opening half-concealed by branches and leaves, was dark and dank enough on a winter evening to supply the faint eeriness, faint dread, without which the sunny hillside might have seemed a little tame. It was, I now know, a very small wood, but it was large enough to feel alone in. To dare oneself to venture into its shadows at twilight, to smell the dank rotting leaves and feel one's feet slipping in the wet earth beside the well, was, for a solitary child, adventure enough. It was not a dread of 'robbers' or even of any ghost from the past that overcame one then, but an older, more primitive fear – half pleasurable, wholly absorbing. It is one of the penalties of growing up that these apprehensions and intuitions gradually become blunted. The wall between us and the other world thickens: what was a constant, if unformulated, awareness, becomes just a memory. It is only very rarely, as the years go on, that a trap-door

185

opens in the memory and a whiff of half-forgotten scents, a glimpse of the mysteries, reaches us once again.

Iris Origo (1902 -)

POLIZIANO

Poliziano the humanist and poet was a close friend of Lorenzo who appointed him tutor to his children.

In order to comprehend (Poliziano's) charm, we must transfer ourselves to Florence on a summer night, when the prince is abroad upon the streets attended by singing-boys as beautiful as Sandro's angels. The professor's chair is forgotten, and Plato's spheres are left to turn unheeded. Pulci and Poliziano join hands with girls from the workshop and the attic. Lorenzo and Pico figure in the dance with prentice-lads and carvers of wood-work or marble. All through the night beneath the stars the music of their lutes is ringing; and when the dancing stops, they gather round some balcony, or hold their own upon the square in matches of improvised melody with the unknown rhymesters of the people. What can be prettier than the ballad of roses made for 'such a night' by Angelo Poliziano?

J. Addington Symonds (1840-93)

I went a-roaming, maidens, one bright day,
In a green garden in mid month of May.

Violets and lilies grew on every side
    Mid the green grass, and young flowers wonderful,
Golden and white and red and azure-eyed;
    Toward which I stretched my hands, eager to pull
    Plenty to make my fair curls beautiful,
To crown my rippling curls with garlands gay.
I went a-roaming, maidens, one bright day,
In a green garden in mid month of May.

But when my lap was full of flowers I spied
    Roses at last, roses of every hue;

Therefore I ran to pluck their ruddy pride,
    Because their perfume was so sweet and true
    That all my soul went forth with pleasure new,
With yearning and desire too soft to say.

I went a-roaming, maidens, one bright day,
In a green garden in mid month of May.

I gazed and gazed. Hard task it were to tell
    How lovely were the roses in that hour:
One was but peeling from her verdant shell,
    And some were faded, some were scarce in flower.
    Then Love said: Go, pluck from the blooming bower
Those that thou seest ripe upon the spray.

I went a-roaming, maidens, one bright day,
In a green garden in mid month of May.

For when the full rose quits her tender sheath,
    When she is sweetest and most fair to see,
Then is the time to place her in thy wreath,
    Before her beauty and her freshness flee.
    Gather ye therefore roses with great glee,
Sweet girls, or e'er their perfume pass away.

I went a-roaming, maidens, one bright day,
In a green garden in mid month of May.

Angelo Poliziano (1454-94)
Translated by J. Addington Symonds (1875)

DIARY

February 10th, I.Tatti

Walking yesterday from Castel di Poggio to Settignano I saw over the ground above the road, oxen slowly dragging the plough between olives and grapevines. It gave me a moment of happiness. Why? The spectacle in itself was beautiful. At the same time it gave me a feeling that

I was looking at what has been going on ever since civilization began, and is likely to go on for a good while yet in Mediterranean lands, where, owing to terracing, the agriculture of the great American and Russian plains would be unsuitable. To think of dragging tractors through a Tuscan terraced *podere!* Then this plowing gave me a sense of continuity as well as hopeful projection into the future, and finally there was something domestic, kindly, *à mesure de l'homme* about it, that I could easily encompass, assimilate, and make my own.

December 7th, I. Tatti

Against a pale, delicate, apple-green sky, getting lighter as you look, the featherlike sickle of the dying moon. So lovely, so calm, so appealing that it is hard to believe what one knows, namely, that what I see and feel and am are meaningless accidents. Hard to believe the contrary, and that it is not a signal, a message to calm, to cheer, to promise, to lift one's heart. Do city dwellers, do the 'hard-boiled', feel as I do, and always have felt, in the presence of nature? You would wish to think so, and the poetry they read and say they enjoy makes you hope they do. Or are they too intent on their greeds to enjoy what one cannot snatch the way a dog does, running away with a bone to consume it undisturbed? If so they do not want our pity. Quite the contrary!

Bernard Berenson (1865-1959)

GEORGIC

As Addington Symonds has noted, Virgil gives a vivid picture of farming life as it must have been in Tuscany although his own farm was actually further south.

Avoid sloping your vineyard towards the setting sun,
And planting hazel among the vines. Never take the highest
Vine-shoots, nor tear your cuttings from the top of a tree
(Such is earth's attraction, the lower do best), nor with blunt blade
Wound the young vines. Don't plant wild olive to support your vines;
For often it happens some careless shepherd lets fall a spark
That, smouldering furtively under their resinous bark at first,
Gets a grip on the wood, leaps out on the leaves aloft,

And roars at the sky; rears up then
In triumph over the branches and crests of the trees, their master,
Rolling the whole plantation in flame, heavenward heaving
A cloud of smoke gross-bodied, greasy and black as pitch –
And worse still if a storm bears down on the wood to marshal
The flames and fan them afar. Should this befall, your vines
Are dead to the roots; you may cut them away, but they'll not recover
Nor awake in green from the earth below as once they did:
Wild olives alone will live there, a barren, bitter stock.
    Let no one, however canny, induce you to work your land
When it's bone-hard under a north wind.
Then icy winter closes down the countryside –
You may cast your seed, but the numb root will never take hold on earth.
The time for setting vines is the first flush of spring
When that white bird arrives, the stork, the bane of serpents;
Or the first frosts of autumn, days when the hotfoot sun
Is not on winter's verge yet, but summer is now passing.
Oh, spring is good for leaves in the spinney, good to forests,
In spring the swelling earth aches for the seed of new life.
Then the omnipotent Father of air in fruitful shower
Comes down to his happy consort
And greatly breeds upon her great body manifold fruit.
Then are the trackless copses alive with the trilling of birds,
And the beasts look for love, their hour come round again:
Lovely the earth in labour, under a tremulous west wind
The fields unbosom, a mild moisture is everywhere.
Confident grows the grass, for the young sun will not harm it;
The shoots of the vine are not scared of a southerly gale arising
Or the sleety rain that slants from heaven beneath a north wind, –
No, bravely now they bud and all their leaves display.
So it was, I believe, when the world first began,
Such the illustrious dawning and tenor of their days.

Virgil (70-19BC)
Translated by C. Day Lewis (1940)

NOVEMBER

The leaves are all now turning to their various shades of yellow, amber, brown, pink and crimson, and autumn has come. Wherever one looks the colours are so brilliant that it seems that this month is even more beautiful than the spring.

The summer people have all drained their swimming pools and bolted their shutters and taken themselves away; and the snakes are going into hibernation though they can still be seen dozing when the sun is warm.

Now there is the smell of woodsmoke from bonfires as the leaves are raked in, and in the evening big fires are lit in the huge open Tuscan fireplaces and chestnuts are roasted and steaks and sausages grilled on the glowing embers.

Raymond Flower (pub. 1978)

HARVEST WOMEN'S SONG

The night is falling and my master sighs:
'Oh, far too short has been the day!' he
  cries.
Well, if 'tis short, some extra let us get,
So go and tell the sun he must not set.
And if 'tis short, the extra must be given:
We'll have to tell the sun to keep in heaven.

Folk Rhyme.

CHAPTER 9

ENCOUNTERS

Vidi madonna sopra un fresco rio
tra verdi frondi e liete donne starsi;
tal che dalla prima ora in qua che io arsi
mai vidi il viso suo più bello e pio.
Questo contentò in parte il mio desio,
e all' alma diè cagion di consolarsi;
ma poi, partendo, il cor vidi restarsi;
crebbon vie più i pensier e 'l dolor mio.
   Chè già il sole inchinava all' occidente,
e lasciava la terra ombrosa e oscura;
onde il mio sole s'ascose in altra parte.
Fe' il primo ben più trista assai la mente:
ah quanto poco al mondo ogni ben dura!
ma il rimembrar si tosto non si parte.

I saw my Lady by a purling brook
With laughing maidens, where green branches twined;
O never since that primal, passionate look
Have I beheld her face so soft and kind.
Hence for a space my yearning was content
And my sad soul some consolation knew;
Alas, my heart remained although I went,
And constantly my pain and sorrow grew.
   Early the sun sank down in western skies
And left the earth to woeful hours obscure,
Afar my sun hath also veiled her ray;
Upon the mind first bliss most heavily lies,
How short a while all mortal joys endure,
But not so soon doth memory pass away.

Lorenzo de Medici (1448-1492)
Translated by Lorna de Lucchi (1922)

A Scuffle

*Benvenuto Cellini was a Florentine goldsmith and sculptor whose memoirs are
amusing as a self portrait and as a picture of Florentine life.*

Having at this time worked with several masters in Florence,
amongst the different goldsmiths I knew in that city, I met with some

persons of worth, as was Marcone, my first master; whilst others, who had the character of honest men, being envious of my works, and robbing and calumniating me, did me the greatest injustice. When I perceived this, I shook off my connections with them, and·looked upon them all as unprincipled men, and little better than thieves.

A goldsmith, amongst the rest, named Giovanni Battista Sogliani, was so complaisant as to lend me part of his shop, which stood at the side of the new market, hard by Landi's bank. There I executed many little works, earned a great deal of money, and was enabled to assist my relations materially. Envy began then to rankle in the hearts of my former bad masters, whose names were Salvadore and Michele Guasconti; they all three kept shops and had immense business. Seeing that they did me ill offices with some men of worth, I complained of it, and said they ought to be satisfied with having robbed me as they had done, under the mask of benevolence. This coming to their ears, they declared loudly that they would make me repent having uttered such words; but I, being a stranger to fear, little regarded their menaces.

As I happened one day to lean against the shop of one of these men, he called me to him, and in the most abusive language bullied and threatened me. Upon which I said, that if they had done their duty with respect to me, I should have spoken of them as persons of fair character; but, as they had behaved in a different manner, they had only themselves to complain of. Whilst I spoke thus, one Gherardo Guasconti, a cousin of theirs, who was in all probability set on by them, took the opportunity, as a beast loaded with bricks happened to pass by, to push it so violently against me, that I was very much hurt. Upon which I instantly turned about and seeing him laugh, gave him so violent a blow on the temple that he fell down, and lay upon the ground motionless and insensible. Then turning to his cousins, I said to them: 'That is the way I use cowardly rascals like you,' and as they, confiding in their number, seemed preparing to take their revenge, I, in a violent passion, drew a little knife, and vented my anger in these words: 'if any one of you offers to quit the shop, let another run for a confessor, as there will be no occasion for a surgeon.' This declaration started such terror into them all, that not one of them ventured to stir to the assistance of his cousin.

Benvenuto Cellini (1500-1571) Translated by T. Roscoe (1822).

It was in Florence on a festa day. What festa? I cannot call to mind. From my window, which looked on to one of the quays of the Arno between the Ponte Santa Trinità and the Ponte Vecchio, I was watching the crowd below, and waiting for the moment towards evening when it becomes more intensely alive, and when I should be seized with the desire to go down and mix with it. And as I was looking up stream, there came a rumour – people began running, and just at the very place on the Ponte Vecchio where the fringe of houses that edge it stops and leaves an empty gap right in the middle of the bridge, I saw the crowd hurrying, bending over the parapet, stretching out their arms and pointing to a small object which was floating away in the muddy waters of the river, disappearing in an eddy, reappearing again, to be finally carried away by the current. I went down. The passers-by I questioned said that a little girl had fallen into the water; her skirt had buoyed her up for a little, but by now she had disappeared. Boats had put out from the shore; men armed with boat-hooks searched the river till nightfall – in vain.

What! in this dense crowd, had there been no-one to notice the child, to hold her back?... I made my way to the Ponte Vecchio. At the very spot from which the little girl had flung herself was a boy about fifteen years old who was answering the questions of the passers-by. He said he had seen the little girl suddenly climb over the balustrade; he had rushed forward and caught her by the arm and for some time had managed to hold her up over the river; the crowds behind him passed on without noticing anything; he had wanted to call for help, as he hadn't the strength to pull the child back on to the bridge by himself. But, 'No!' she had said, 'let me go,' and in such a heart-rending voice that in the end he had loosed his hold. He sobbed as he told his story.

(He himself was one of those poor children who would perhaps be less unhappy without a family. He was dressed in rags. And I imagined that at the moment he was holding the little girl by the arm and trying to wrest her from death, feeling and sharing her despair, a despairing love had seized him too as it had her, and had opened Heaven for them both. It was out of pity he had let go. 'Prego...lasciatemi.')

People asked him whether he knew her; but no; it was the first time he had seen her; no-one knew who she was and all the enquiries made in the days following were fruitless. The body was found. It was that of a girl of fourteen; very thin, and dressed in very wretched clothes. What

Botticelli (1444-1510), detail from Venus and Mars   National Gallery London

would I not have given to know more about her – whether her father had a mistress or her mother a lover, and what support had suddenly failed her without which she was unable to live.

'But why,' Nathanial asked me, 'this story in a book you dedicate to joy?'

I wish I could have told this story more simply still. Truly, I do not want a happiness that springs from wretchedness. Riches that leave another poor I do not want. If my clothes are stripped from others, I will go naked. Ah! Lord Christ, your table is open to all, and what makes the beauty of your banquet is that all are invited to it.

André Gide (1869-1951)
Translated by D. Bussey (1949)

A PARTY

Harriet Beaujolois Campell was probably still under 14 when she wrote her vivid descriptions of social life in Florence.

Last Saturday Walter gave his ball here. Every body thought it splendid and all in all it was so for this country. More than half the people Italians I mean did not come. But we had quite enough for the size of the room. It began neare ten, and from that moment till three I never stopped dancing in consequence I am quite stiff and soar but I enjoyed myself exceedingly. The Duc de Berry made love to Eleanor as much as ever but all in vain for he is married to a pretty little woman and Eleanor will soon be so to Uxbridge. He wrote to her the other day in the greatest despair having heard that she was to be married to Lord Ancram immediately. He will shortly be of age and then no impediment remains. Lord Anglesey's displeasure will signify little. She has had an affair too with Mr. Chumley but she refused him point blank telling him she was engaged. In consequence he has not appeared for some time and I even believe he is gone.

We expect Eliza in a few days on her road to Naples. Her health is still bad but if any thing can do her good it would be the warm air we enjoy here every day. I have never yet passed so delightful a November. No where but Italy could one enjoy so great a blessing. And yet this country with all the charms of climate the fine arts and the richness and beauty of nature bears but weakly a comparison to England. Nature is in perfection but mankind is so degraded by vice

197

that people of a better nation tremble at the recital of their dreadful lives. And with all these feelings which I believe are innate in a Briton's breast unpolluted by foreign wickedness human nature is ever too weak to withstand the dangerous charms of luxurious sin. I often half envy the happy life of an Italian free from care and brought up so as to be almost devoid of conscience enjoying the finest country as to country devoid of men perhaps in the world, indulging in every inclination natural to man loving to be loved and all without restraint. Yes I sigh after such happiness. I fancy myself such a being and the dearest illusion is maddenning and delightful again. When I think upon the English, and consider how inestimably good they are what sound happiness they enjoy I am proud of forming a part though so small of such a nation. Yet human nature is ever weak and my young heart would soon yeild to the love of a member of this curious race of beings.

Harriet Beaujolois Campbell (1803-1864)

A version of the curious love story of Ginevra and Antonio was told by Boccaccio, and is supposed to be based on fact.

Antonio Rondinelli, having fallen in love with Ginevra degli Amieri, could not by any means obtain her from her father, who preferred to give her to Francesco Agolanti, because he was of noble family. The grief of Rondinelli cannot be described, but it was equalled by that of Ginevra, who could never be reconciled to the marriage which was arranged for her. Whether, therefore, from a struggle with hopeless love, or from hysteria, or some other cause, it is a fact that, after this ill-assorted marriage had lasted for four years, Ginevra fell into an unconscious state, and, after remaining without pulse or sign of life for some time, was believed to be dead, and as such was buried in the family tomb in the cemetery of the Duomo near the Campanile. The death of Ginevra, however, was not real, but an appearance produced by catalepsy. The night after her interment she returned to conscious-ness, and, perceiving what had happened, contrived to unfasten her hands, and crept as well as she could up the little steps of the vault, and, having lifted the stone, came forth. Then, by the shortest way, called Via della Morta from this circumstance, she went to her husband's house in the Corso degli Adimari; but, not being received by him, who from her feeble voice and white dress believed her to be a spectre, she went to the house of Bernardo Amieri, her father, who lived in the

Mercato Vecchio behind S.Andrea, and then to that of an uncle who lived close by, where she received the same repulse.

Giving in to her unhappy fate, it is said that she then took refuge under the loggia of S.Bartolommeo in the Via Calzaioli, where, while praying that death would put an end to her misery, she remembered her beloved Rondinelli, who had always proved faithful to her. To him she found her way, was kindly received and cared for, and in a few days restored to her former health.

Up to this point the story has nothing incompatible with truth, but that which is difficult to believe is the second marriage of Ginevra with Antonio Rondinelli, while her first husband was still living, and her petition to the Ecclesiastical Tribunals, who decided, that the first marriage having been dissolved by death, the lady might legitimately accept another husband.

Giovanni Boccaccio (1313-1375)
Translated by A. Hare (c. 1875)

FALLING IN LOVE

Vittorio Alfieri the Italian dramatist fell passionately in love with Louise of Stolberg, the wife of Bonnie Prince Charlie of Scotland, then living in Florence. Alfieri and Louise moved into what is now the British Consulate, by the Arno and lived there together for many years.

During the preceding summer, which I passed at Florence, I had frequently seen a beautiful, amiable, and very distinguished foreigner. It was impossible not to meet and remark this lady, and still more impossible to fail to admire her. Though a great number of the Florentine nobility, as well as most foreigners of distinction, visited at her house, yet being always anxious, owing to my reserved and backward character, to avoid the society of beautiful and accomplished females, I declined an introduction and contented myself with meeting her at the theatres and public walks. The first impression she made on me was infinitely agreeable. Large black eyes full of fire and sweetness, joined to a fair complexion and hair, gave to her beauty a brilliancy it was difficult to withstand. Twenty-five years of age, possessing a taste for letters and the fine arts, an amiable character, an immense fortune, yet placed in domestic circumstances of a very painful nature, how was it possible to escape where so many reasons existed for loving her?

During the autumn one of my friends offered several times to introduce me at her house. I believed myself sufficiently fortified against feminine charms, but I was soon unconsciously caught in the toils of love. Still irresolute whether to resist or yield to this new passion, I took post in the month of December and proceeded to Rome. This foolish and fatiguing journey gave rise to my sonnet on Rome which I composed in a wretched inn at Baccano where I could not shut my eyes all night. This journey occupied me only twelve days. Both in going and returning I passed through Siena and visited my friend Gori who did not disapprove of the new chains which he perceived I was forging for myself, so that they became strongly riveted on my return to Florence. This fourth and last passion was marked by very different symptoms from the others. In the three former the mind had no share, but in the present instance a sentiment of esteem, mingling with love, rendered this passion, if less impetuous, at least more profound and durable. Such was the love which henceforward animated and held dominion over my mind, and which will only terminate with my existence. I soon perceived that the object of my present attachment, far from impeding my progress in the pursuit of useful knowledge or deranging my studies like the frivolous females with whom I was formerly enamoured, urged me on by her example to everything dignified and praise-worthy. Having once learned to know and appreciate so rare and valuable a friend I yielded myself up entirely to her influence. I was not mistaken; for twelve years afterwards, at this present moment as I sit scribbling these pages at an age when the illusion of passions have ceased to operate, I feel that I become daily more attached to her in proportion as time destroys the brilliancy of her inevitably fleeting beauty, the only charm which is not intrinsic. Whenever I reflect on her virtues my soul is elevated, improved and tranquillized and I dare to affirm that her feelings which I have uniformly endeavoured to fortify and confirm are not dissimilar to my own.

Vittorio Alfieri (1749-1803)
Translated by E.R.P. Vincent (1961)

MILTON AND GALILEO AT VILLA ARCETRI

Milton and Galileo met briefly in Arcetri outside Florence.

'There unseen
In manly beauty Milton stood before him

Gazing with reverent awe – Milton – his guest,
Just come forth, all life and enterprise;
He in his old age and extremity,
Blind, at noonday exploring with his staff;
His eyes upturned as to the golden sun,
His eyeballs idly rolling. Little then
Did Galileo think whom he received;
That in his hand he held the hand of one
Who could requite him – who would spread his name
O'er lands and seas – great as himself, nay, greater;
Milton as little that in him he saw,
As in a glass, what he himself should be,
Destined so soon to fall on evil days
And evil tongues – so soon – alas, to live
In darkness, and with dangers compassed round,
And solitude.'

Samuel Rogers (1763-1855)

Maxim Gorki (1868-1936) became famous in Florence for his original dinner parties.

Gorki's presence soon became popular in Florence. Maria Andreievna used to say: 'In Naples the people who recognise him smile and bow to him. In Florence they point at him: nothing but that.'
    At his house one used to meet Russians and Poles – extremely original people, at least for us Italians and our pedestrian habits. A Pole, whose name I do not recall, was always dining with Gorki: black hair, black nails, black morning-coat, without a shirt, with only a starched shirt-front which escaped from the opening of his waist-coat at every moment, revealing his bare chest. He was a poet, and I deeply regret that I have forgotten his glorious name. One evening I was sitting next to him at table. The soup passed, the fish passed, and the waiter always forgot me, and with me he forgot my neighbour as well. Smilingly, I called Maria Andreievna's attention, and she calmly answered: 'Excuse us, but your neighbour never eats, he only drinks, and the waiter must have thought that you have the same habits.' In fact I saw the poet again at the Gorkis' several times, and never did I see him eat so much as a biscuit, so steadfastly did he adhere to his tenets: I did, indeed, see him drink, but red wine only, a whole glass at

a time. I still desire to read his poetry, and I wonder if he is still alive?

There was also Anatole Lunacharsky, a man of great learning and of an astounding memory for all that concerns European literature. He had, a short time before, published essays in critical philosophy; he was then writing a book on religion, and was preparing with Gorki a history of Russian literature. He spoke excellent French and also a passable Italian. But, during those days, according to what the Gorkis told us, he was worrying because his wife, after the completion of the ninth month, had been confined to bed for four weeks in the vain expectation of a baby. They would both of them have been extremely happy had their baby been born in Florence; and this was certainly a compliment for us all. At last one day, after endless waiting, I met Lunacharsky with his excellent wife, a nice round rosy little woman, with a little red felt hat crossed by a white pigeon's feather, in the Piazza Vittorio Emanuele, and I approached to congratulate them. 'Not at all', Lunacharsky said with a sigh: *'Elle s'est levée en désespoir de cause.'* I often think of Madam Lunacharsky when I read the news of the Russian revolution.

Ugo Ojetti (1919-)
Translated by H. Furst (1928)

A VISIT TO THE BROWNINGS

Florence, June 9th, Wednesday.

Mamma, Miss Shepard, and I, went last evening, at eight o'clock, to see the Brownings; and after some search and inquiry, we found the Casa Guidi, which is a palace in a street not very far from our own... He (Browning) came into the ante-room to greet us; as did his little boy, Robert, whom they nickname Penny for fondness. This latter cognomen is a diminutive of Apennine, which was bestowed upon him at his first advent into the world, because he was so very small; there being a statue in Florence nicknamed Apennine, because it is so huge. I never saw such a boy as this before; so slender, fragile, and spritelike, not as if he were actually in ill-health, but as if he had little or nothing to do with human flesh and blood. His face is very pretty and most intelligent, and exceedingly like his mother's, whose constitutional lack of stamina I suppose he inherits. He is nine years old, and seems at once less childlike and less manly than would befit that age. I should not quite like to be the father of such a boy; and should fear to stake so much interest and affection on him as he cannot fail to inspire. I wonder what is to become of him; – whether he will ever grow to be a man; – whether it is desirable that he should. His parents ought to turn their whole attention to making him gross and earthy, and giving him a thicker scabbard to sheathe his spirit in. He was born in Florence, and prides himself on being a Florentine and indeed as un-English a production as if he were native of another planet.

Mrs Browning met us at the door of the drawing-room and greeted us most kindly; a pale little woman, scarcely bodied at all; at any rate, only substantial enough to put her slender fingers to be grasped and to speak with a soft yet sweet, tenuity of voice. Really, I do not see how Browning can suppose that he has an earthly wife, any more than an earthly child; both are of the elfin-breed, and will away from him, some day, when he least thinks of it. She is a good and kind fairy, however, and sweetly disposed toward the human race, although only remotely akin to it. It is wonderful to see how small she is; how diminutive, and peaked, as it were her face, without being ugly; how pale her cheek; how brown and dark her eyes. There is not such another figure in the world; and her black ringlets cluster down into her neck and make her face look the whiter by their sable profusion and I could not form any judgment about her age; it may range from anywhere within the limits of human life, or elfin-life. When we met her in London, at Mr. Milnes's breakfast-table, she did not impress me so strangely; for the morning light is more prosaic than the dim illumination of their great, tapestried drawing-room; and besides, sitting next to her, she did not then have occasion to raise her voice in speaking, and I was not sensible what a slender pipe she has. It is as if a grasshopper should speak. It is marvellous to me how so extraordinary, so acute, so sensitive a creature, can impress us, as she does, with the certainty of her benevolence. It seems to me there were a million chances to one that she would have been a miracle of acidity and bitterness.

We were not the only guests. Mr. & Mrs. Eckers, Americans, recently from the East, and on intimate terms with the Brownings, arrived after us, also Miss Fanny Howarth, an English literary lady, whom I have met several times in Liverpool and lastly came the white head and palmer-like beard of Mr. Bryant, with his daughter. Mr. Browning was very efficient in keeping up conversation with everybody, and seemed to be in all parts of the room and in every group at the same moment; a most vivid and quick-thoughted person, logical and common-sensible, as I presume poets generally are, in their daily talk.

We had some tea and some strawberries, and passed a pleasant evening. There was no very noteworthy conversation; the most interesting topic being that disagreeable, and now wearisome one of spiritual communications, as regards which Mrs. Browning is a believer, and her husband an infidel. I am rather surprised that Browning's conversation should be so clear, and so much to the purpose of the moment; since his poetry can seldom proceed far without running into the high grass of latent meanings and obscure allusions.

Mrs. Browning's health does not permit late hours; so we began to take leave at about ten o'clock. I heard her ask Mr. Bryant if he did not mean to re-visit Europe, and heard him answer, not uncheerfully taking hold of his white hair, 'It is getting rather too late in the evening now.' If any old age can be cheerful, I should think his might be; so good a man, so cool, so calm – so bright, too, we may say – his life has been like the days that end in pleasant sunsets. He has a great loss, however – or what ought to be a great loss – soon to be encountered in the death of his wife, who, I think, can hardly live to reach America. He is not eminently an affectionate man. I take him to be one who cannot get closely home to his sorrow, nor feel it so sensibly as he gladly would; and in consequence of that deficiency, the world lacks substance to him. It is partly the result, perhaps, of his not having sufficiently cultivated his animal and emotional nature; his poetry shows it, and his personal intercourse – though kindly – does not stir one's blood in the least.

Little Penny, during the evening, sometimes helped the guests to cake and strawberries, joined in the conversation when he had anything to say, or sat down upon a couch to enjoy his own meditations. He has long curling hair, and has not yet emerged from his frock and drawers. It is funny to think of putting him into breeches. His likeness to his mother is strange to behold.

Nathaniel Hawthorne (1804-1864)

BERNARD BERENSON

The art historian Bernard Berenson was lionized by the literary and artistic circles in Tuscany. He and his villa, I Tatti, were also a focal point for many English and American travellers in Europe.

This strength of mind was chained to a physical fragility that was quite frightening at times. It was not that his sight or hearing failed – they remained unusually good almost to the very end – but those delicate blue-veined hands had the translucency of porcelain, he was as thin as a ghost and altogether too light and buoyant; one puff of wind, it seemed, might blow him away. And indeed after I had left Florence he had a fearful accident. He was standing on top of an embankment admiring a view when a buffet of wind slammed the car door upon him and he lost his footing. Down the embankment he went, rolling over and over like a piece of thistledown until at last he came to rest inert and unconscious at the bottom. And yet he lived. There was something in his very fragility that preserved him. In the upheaval of the war and its aftermath most of his contemporaries died, but like the one piece of brittle china that miraculously escapes the blast in a bombed house he continued to live on.

...Nor would it have been difficult to criticize the house itself. Much of the furniture was lumpish and even ugly, and the rooms were too small and dark. There were of course beautiful objects in every corner, but perhaps there were too many of them for a house that was not yet a museum. I remember one night being there alone – the family had gone up to the hills at Vallombrosa and the servants were in their own rooms at the rear – and I inadvertently switched out all the lights. By no amount of groping on the wall could I find the switches again and so there was nothing for it but to make my way to the front door some fifty yards away in total darkness. Ornaments and glass shelves filled with breakable *objets d'art* lay, I knew, on every side, and after the first few steps I lost my nerve. I dropped to my hands and knees and inch by inch edged my way along the corridors, every instant portending some terrible crash, until at last like a cat-burglar I found the door and escaped into the night.

Alan Moorehead (1910-83)

D'ANNUNZIO

Gabriele D'Annunzio the poet and playwright was always a controversial figure because of his political views and the eroticism in some of his work. D'Annunzio had many lovers.

Arrived at Borgo San Dannino, stormy sky. I find Amaranta at the station, trembling all over and afraid. I was not expecting her. She was

205

wearing her black silk costume and the hat with a feather. Agitated conversation on the square. In terror, flashes of love. We climb into the carriage. I speak in that low, rather rough voice which upsets her. So as not to hear it, she covers her ears with a crazy gesture. We stop at a little inn called 'The Roman Eagle'. We are given a room with an enormous bed. Feverish caresses interrupted by her childish agitation. Slight taste of iodine on her white skin. The body is still marvellous and my desire still frantic. A meal is brought which we do not touch. She wants to return to Salsa. After long kisses we go down the wooden staircase. On the square, a concert of guitars and mandolins. A cold wind has made a stormy sky. The carriage is drawn by a white horse. The wind blows her veil, through which I seek her mouth. Under the street-lamps I see her terrified face. It is raining. Sadness. Sadness. Why did I let her leave? She goes back into her hotel and takes the two boxes of orchids. I find my bed impregnated with her odour; impossible to sleep... How exquisite and yet trivial life is. I keep the inn bill. So much intoxication and so much anguish has cost only twenty-one lire.

Gabriele D'Annunzio (1863-1938)
Translated by S. Hardman (1972)

CHAPTER 10

PANE E VINO

For July, in Siena, by the willow-tree,
  I give you barrels of white Tuscan wine
  In ice far down your cellars stored supine;
And morn and eve to eat in company
Of those vast jellies dear to you and me;
  Of partridges and youngling pheasants sweet,
  Boiled capons, sovereign kids: and let their treat
Be veal and garlic, with whom these agree.
Let time slip by, till by-and-by, all day;
  And never swelter through the heat at all,
But move at ease at home, sound, cool, and gay;
  And wear sweet-coloured robes that lightly fall;
And keep your tables set in fresh array,
  Not coaxing spleen to be your seneschal.

Folgore da San Gemignano (c.13-14)
Translated by Dante Gabriel Rossetti (1828-1882)

MONTEPULCIANO

What we were doing, or what we expected to do, at Montepulciano I keep no other trace of than is bound up in a present quite tender consciousness that I wouldn't for the world not have been there. I think my reason must have been largely just in the beauty of the name (for could any beauty be greater?), reinforced no doubt by the fame of the local vintage and the sense of how we should quaff it on the spot. Perhaps we quaffed it too constantly; since the romantic picture reduces itself for me but to two definite appearances; that of the more priggish discrimination so far reasserting itself as to advise me that Montepulciano was dirty, even remarkably dirty; and that of its being not much else besides but perched and brown and queer and crooked, and noble withal (which is what almost any Tuscan city more easily than not acquits herself of): all the while she may on such occasions figure, when one looks off from her to the end of dark street-vistas or catches glimpses through high arcades, some big battered, blistered, overladen, overmasted ship, swimming in a violet sea.

Henry James (1843-1916)

Piero della Francesca (1410-1492), Visit of the Queen of Sheba to Solomon (detail)
St Francis Arezzo (Photo Alinari)

The oldest red wine in Tuscany is made in the province of Siena and bears the name of Brunello di Montalcino. The first documents about it date back to the 8th century, when the Lombards were masters of the region. This wine must be aged in special wooden barrels for at least four years; otherwise it cannot be bottled as Brunello. One of its exceptional features is that it continues to age indefinitely in the bottle, and its flavour becomes better and more velvety as the years pass. It is made with only one type of grape, the *brunello,* is produced in limited quantities in a very restricted zone and is bottled by very few producers.

...The area that produces the wine known as Chianti Classico lies between the cities of Florence and Siena. It is the oldest of the Chianti zones, and its traditional trademark is a black cock on a field of yellow-gold, a symbol taken from an *affresco* painted by Vasari on a ceiling of the Palazzo Vecchio in Florence. The producers who have a right to use this trademark are limited by geographic position and by the severe standards of the *Consorzio del Gallo Nero,* established in 1924.

Wilma Pezzini (pub. 1978)

MARTINMAS IN THE TUSCAN MAREMMA

Grey mists climb the shaggy hills,
Fall in rain upon their crest,
'Neath the wind from the North-West
Bellows and whitens the sea.

But from wine that seethes in vats,
Through the town in ev'ry street
Floating odours pungent sweet
Fill all men's hearts with glee.

Sputt'ring loud with heat the spit
Turns above the glowing brands;
At his door the huntsman stands
Whistling, watches, o'er the lea.

'Gainst clouds of sombre rose relieved,
Flocks of birds dark plumaged stream;

211

How like exile thoughts that seem
Toward the setting sun to flee.

Giosué Carducci (1835-1907)
Translated by G.H. Greene (1893)

DECEMBER: a time of short days when one has to make the most of each hour of daylight. This is when the other main product of Chianti – the olives – are ripe and the *contadini* are everywhere busy gathering with ladders and parachutes spread on the ground to catch the crop. There is not the same festive spirit about this as there is for the *vendemmia* – olive-picking is tedious, cold work. The olives are small and hard and it does not seem possible they will yield so much oil.

Despite the short days, winter has not really started yet, and there are still a few determined flowers; pale roses linger on in the garden and there are scabious and marguerites and always the wild marigolds – it is said that if they are still closed at 7 a.m. it will rain during the day.

Now too there is much chopping of wood, and one hears the sound of the mechanical saws as logs are cut. Everywhere there are huge stacks of wood which wait until they are seasoned and ready to burn. Much wood is burnt in the winter in the big hearths and the local people refer sometimes to Christmas as 'Ceppo' – meaning log.

Raymond Flower (pub. 1978)

La prima oliva e oro, la seconda argento, la terza mon val niente.
(The best olive is gold, the second silver, the third is worth nothing.)

Tuscan Saying

14TH CENTURY COOKING

Both meat and fish were almost always served with rich sauces and well stuffed; indeed it is perhaps the contemplation of these sauces and spices which – more than anything else in these papers – opens an alarming gulf between the Datinis and ourselves. What appetites they must have had – and what digestions! Three of the most popular sauces for everyday use were a red one called *savore sanguigno,* made of raisins, cinnamon, sandal, and sumach (a substance now used only for tanning) pounded together and mixed with meat and wine; a sauce called *peverata*, made of meat, fish, pepper, cinnamon, ginger, and nutmeg and coloured with saffron; and a white sauce called *camellina,* made of sugar, cinnamon, cloves, bread, and vinegar. And at banquets there were sauces containing not only many other spices, but also precious stones or gold and pearls. As for the stuffing – the more varied the ingredients, the finer the dish! Not only chickens and partridges and peacocks but even veal, mutton, and wild boar were stuffed with a mixture of sugar, fats, spices, onion, garlic, and pounded almonds. Above all, no banquet was complete without a *torta* – the 'grete pie' of English medieval cooking – a dish which ingeniously evaded the sumptuary law against the serving of more than three courses, by putting both meats and sweets in the same dish. One of these *torte* – whose recipe is given in the *Libro della cucina del secola XIV* – contained pork, chickens, ham, sausages, onions, parsley, dates, almonds, flour, cheese, eggs, sugar, salt, saffron, and several other spices. First the chickens were fried in oil, then the ham was made into *ravioli*, and then chickens, sausages, and *ravioli* were laid on layers of pastry, alternating with layers of dates and almonds. The pie was then covered with pastry, and cooked in hot embers. And there is also, in the same book, a fascinating recipe for 'a pie with live birds' – in which live song-birds were put into a pie of which the roof had little windows – the whole pie being then hung on a tree of pastry. 'Wasn't that a dainty dish to set before a king?'

Iris Origo (1902-)

The Tuscans are Italy's keenest hunters. On the first day of the shooting season the whole region explodes. Pheasants, hares, and even larks and thrushes become victims of this passion, the only good result of which is superb game recipes, like the following one for homemade pasta.

Pappardelle with hare
Pappardelle are very broad noodles (about 1 inch wide) with ruffled edges. They are cut with a fluted pastry wheel from a flat sheet of pasta which has been allowed to dry only briefly.

For 6 persons

Homemade pappardelle made with 3 eggs and 2¼ cups (300 gr.) all-purpose (plain) flour

the front legs of a hare
1 small onion, finely chopped
1 carrot, finely chopped
1 stick of celery, chopped
2 tablespoons parsley, chopped
2 teaspoons all-purpose (plain) flour
1 cup red wine
1 cup stock or water
1 or 2 cloves garlic, finely chopped
2 tablespoons olive oil (good corn oil would do)
6 tablespoons (90 gr.) butter
1 ounce (30 gr.) streaky bacon, chopped (preferably unsmoked)
2 tablespoons heavy (double) cream
a pinch of grated nutmeg
a small sprig of rosemary
salt and freshly ground black pepper

1. Sauté the bacon in the oil and 4 tablespoons (60 gr.) of the butter. Add the onion and cook for a few minutes, until it is transparent. Add the carrot, celery, garlic, and rosemary and sauté for a further 5 minutes.

2. Add the hare legs and brown them on all sides. Add flour, and brown, stirring rapidly. Add the wine, raise heat, and cook until the liquid has reduced by half. Add the cream and nutmeg. Mix well and adjust seasoning. Add ½ cup of water or stock. The sauce should be rather thick. Reduce heat, cover, and cook for a good hour, stirring occasionally and adding the remaining water or stock during the cooking.

3. Remove the hare legs from the pan. Bone

them and cut the meat into small pieces. Return the meat to the sauce, and keep it hot.

4. Cook and drain the *pappardelle*. Toss them with the remaining butter, turn them into a hot serving dish, and cover with the sauce. Mix well, sprinkle with parsley, and serve.

In Tuscany this dish is served without cheese, but some Parmesan could be served on the side, if desired.

Anna del Conte (pub. 1976)

There are *two* Italies – one composed of the green earth and transparent sea, and the mighty ruins of ancient time, and the aereal mountains, and the warm and radiant atmosphere which is interfused through all things. The other consists of the Italians of the present day, their works and ways. The one is the most sublime and lovely contemplation that can be conceived by the imagination of man; the other is the most degraded, disgusting and odious. What do you think? Young women of rank actually eat – you will never guess what – *garlick!*

Percy Bysshe Shelley (1792-1822)

ROSEMARY, FOURTEENTH CENTURY

Rosemary, with which the delicious *pan di ramerino,* still beloved by Tuscan children, was made, was considered almost miraculous in its efficacy, since it possessed no less than twenty-six 'noble and admirable properties' including those of curing colds, toothache, aching feet, bad breath, sweat, lack of appetite, gout, consumption, and madness! In addition, 'if you would keep your face beautiful and clear, take rosemary and boil its leaves in pure white wine and wash in it'. And 'if you put rosemary leaves under your bed, it will keep you from evil dreams'. And finally, 'if you plant rosemary in your garden or

215

vineyard or orchard, your vines and fruit will grow in great abundance, and it will delight your eyes when they fall upon it.

Iris Origo (1902-)

A PRESCRIPTION

Lorenzo suffered, like many of his family, from gout.

First, and before anything else, you must purge yourself before the spring, that is before the middle of March, and after that, if you feel any pain, you must anoint yourself with the ointment made as I told Messer Aldovrandino, who will give you the recipe. When you have done this, the pain will cease, if it ever came on, but if it does not come on, you could all the same take some medicine which would purge you of the evil matter. My medicine is in solid form, and is called Ellescof, and you must take half an ounce in the morning, at sunrise, and do this once a month, especially when you feel the pain. In addition to this, so that it shall not return, you should have a stone, called heliotrope, mounted in a gold ring in such a way that it can touch the skin, and wear it on the ring finger of the left hand. If you do this, the gout and arthritic pains will never return, for it has hidden properties and a special form, which prevents the humours from going to the joints. For I am an expert in such things, and this is divine and miraculous. After that, in the summer, in the month of August, I will find a red stone which is born in the belly of a swallow and I will send it to you. You must wrap it in linen, and sew it in your shirt, under the left breast, where it will act in the same way as the aforesaid heliotrope. And thus, God willing, you will be free and safe from any pains in your joints. Messer Aldovrandino will tell you about this, and explain at length. But in order that you may know the future, I send you my forecast for the year 1488, enclosed with this.

Lorenzo de Medici's physician (15th century)
Translated by Y. Maguire (1936)

PAOLO UCCELLO (1397-1475)

Uccello also did some work in *terra verde* and colour in the cloister of San Miniato outside Florence. He painted scenes from the lives of the

Fathers of the Church, in which he ignored the rule of consistency in colouring, for he made the fields blue, the cities red, and the buildings in various colours as he felt inclined. He was wrong to do so, because something which is meant to represent stone cannot and should not be coloured with another tint. It is said that while Paolo was at work on this painting the abbot gave him for his meals hardly anything but cheese. Paolo grew sick of this, but being a mild-mannered man he merely decided not to go there anymore. The abbot sent to look for him, but whenever Paolo heard the friars asking for him he arranged not to be at home. And if he happened to meet a pair of them in Florence he took to his heels as fast as he could in the opposite direction. Seeing this, two of them who were more curious than the rest (and could run faster) caught him up one day and demanded why he never returned to finish the work he had started and why he always ran away when he caught sight of a friar. Paolo said:

'You've brought me to such a sorry state that I not only run away from the sight of you, I can't even go where there are carpenters working. This is all the fault of your dim-witted abbot. What with his cheese pies and his cheese soups, he's stuffed me so full of cheese that I'm frightened they'll use me to make glue. If he went on any more I wouldn't be Paolo Uccello, I'd be pure cheese.'

The friars roared with laughter and went and told the abbot what Uccello said; and then the abbot persuaded him to come back and gave him something else for his meals.

Giorgio Vasari (1511-74)
Translated by G. Bell (1965)

Of the Florentines, though most courteous, yet sparing, other Italians jeast, saying, that when they meete a man about dinner time, they aske Vos' Signoria ha desinato, Sir, have you dined? and if he answer, I, they replie, as if they would have invited him to dinner: but if he answere no, they reply Andate Signor, ch'e otta, Goe Sir, for it is high time to dine. They thinke it best to cherish and increase friendship by metings in Market places and Gardens, but hold the table and bed unfit for conversation, where men should come to eate quickly, and sleepe soundly.

Fynes Moryson (1566-1617?)

In the Middle Ages, during periods of famine, *castagne*, chestnuts, in all forms, were a staple food. In the Tuscan mountains habits and memories of those days still prevail, and chestnuts are dried and reduced to flour now, even as they were a long time ago. The resulting product is called *farina dolce*, sweet flour, and it was once an important part of the winter diet of the marble workers in the Garfagnana mountains. They used it as a base for a cheap and nourishing gruel, *polenta di castagne*, which was eaten, whenever possible, with *biroldo*, a Tuscan pork sausage made with the ears, cartilage, fat and blood of the animal and spiced with pepper, nutmeg, cloves and coriander. Some manufacturers add raisins. These two substantial dishes were naturally washed down with plenty of good local wine.

Chestnut flour is still in use today. In Florence they make a good flat cake out of it, called *castagnaccio*, which is covered with *pinoli* nuts and scented with rosemary leaves, and then eaten with creamy *ricotta* cheese.

CASTAGNACCIO *(Chestnut Flour Cake)*

Serves 6 to 8

2 tablespoons raisins
4 cups chestnut flour
6 tablespoons olive oil
3 tablespoons sugar
1½ teaspoons salt
2 cups water
Butter, as needed
Bread crumbs, as needed
1 sprig fresh rosemary, or 1½ teaspoons dried
2 tablespoons pinoli nuts

Preheat oven to 400°F. Cover raisins with warm water. Sift the flour into a large bowl, add olive oil, sugar and salt. Stir well, then slowly add the water, always mixing with a wooden spoon. The result should be a semi-liquid batter.

Sodoma (1477-1549), Detail from fresco at Monte Oliveto Maggiore
Monte Oliveto Maggiore (Photo Alinari)

Butter a cake pan, sprinkle it with bread crumbs. Drain the raisins. Remove the rosemary leaves from sprig and chop them coarse. Pour the batter into the cake pan, sprinkle with *pinoli* nuts, raisins and rosemary.

Bake for 40 to 50 minutes, until a light crust is formed on top and a toothpick stuck into the middle comes out dry. Serve hot or cold.

Marcella Hazan (pub. 1973)

Piero, Lorenzo's eldest son, had a sweet tooth. He sent this missive to his father when he was probably about 5 years old.

A letter to Lorenzo

Please send me some figs, for I like them. I mean those red ones, and some peaches with stones, and other things you know I like, sweets and cakes and other little things, as you think best. We are at Trebbio and Madonna Ginēvra, who spoils us...

Piero de Medici (1471-1503)
Translated by Y. Maguire (1936)

The Tuscans, particularly the Florentines, have always loved broad beans.

MINESTRA DI FAVE

For 6 persons:

4 ounces (125 gr.) small macaroni
1 large onion, cut in rings
2 cloves garlic, chopped
1 pound (500 gr.) fresh shelled young broad beans, or frozen or canned broad beans
5 cups light chicken stock or 2 to 4 chicken bouillon cubes

dissolved in 5 cups of water
5 tablespoons olive oil
2 tablespoons concentrated tomato paste
1 bay leaf
2 tablespoons ricotta or cottage cheese
Salt and freshly ground black pepper

Sauté the onions and garlic in the oil for 5 minutes. Add the tomato paste and the bay leaf and fry for 1 minute. Add the broad beans, and fry for 2 minutes, stirring constantly. Cover with the stock and adjust seasoning, and cook for about 10 minutes.

When the broad beans are cooked, remove bay leaf, lift approximately half of the broad beans out of the pan with a slotted spoon and put them on a plate. Peel them. Also lift out as many onion rings as possible and add them to the peeled broad beans.

Purée the rest of the soup. Return it to the saucepan, add the pasta and boil gently until it is cooked. Add the peeled broad beans, the onion rings and ricotta. Stir over low heat for 1 minute. Serve. A bowl of grated Parmesan cheese can be served on the side, if desired.

Anna del Conte (pub. 1976)

Fiorentin mangia fagiuoli
Lecca piatti e tovaglioli.

The Florentine who eats beans
licks the plates and tableclothes.

Florentine saying

Sketch by Leonardo da Vinci (1452-1519) Victoria and Albert Museum Crown ©

CHAPTER 11

ENDINGS

'Avevo un fiorellino, mi s'e appasito;
Avevo un cuore, e me l'hanno rubato;
Avevo un damo, e questo m'ha tradito!

I had a little flower, I saw it fade;
I had a heart, t'was stolen from my breast:
I had a love, and me he has betrayed.

Tuscan folk rhyme

O sun that sinkest low, that sinkest low;
That goest down behind the hills away;
Do me one favour, sun, as thou dost go:
Salute my love, we have not met to-day.
O sun, just setting where those pear trees rise,
Salute for me, I pray thee, those black eyes.
O sun, behind the poplars lost to sight,
Salute those eyes so beautiful and bright.

Roadside Song
Translated by Francesca Alexander (1859)

ANDREA DEL SARTO (1486-1531)

I often am much wearier than you think
This evening more than usual, and it seems
As if – forgive now – should you let me sit
Here by the window with your hand in mine
And look a half-hour forth on Fiesole,
Both of one mind, as married people use,
Quietly, quietly the evening through,
I might get up tomorrow to my work
Cheerful and fresh as ever. Let us try.
Tomorrow, how you shall be glad for this!
Your soft hand is a woman of itself,
And mine the man's bared breast she curls inside.
Don't count the time lost, neither; you must serve

For each of the five pictures we require:
It saves a model. So! keep looking so –
My serpentining beauty, rounds on rounds!
– How could you ever prick those perfect ears,
Even to put the pearl there! oh, so sweet –
My face, my moon, my everybody's moon,
Which everybody looks on and calls his,
And, I suppose, is looked on by in turn,
While she looks – no one's: very dear, no less.
You smile? why, there's my picture ready made,
There's what we painters call our harmony!
A common greyness silvers everything, –
All in a twilight, you and I alike
– You, at the point of your first pride in me
(That's gone you know), – but I, at every point;
My youth, my hope, my art, being all toned down
To yonder sober pleasant Fiesole.
There's the bell clinking from the chapel-top;
That length of convent-wall across the way
Holds the trees safer, huddled more inside;
The last monk leaves the garden; days decrease,
And autumn grows, autumn in everything.
Eh? the whole seems to fall into a shape
As if I saw alike my work and self
And all that I was born to be and do,
A twilight-piece. Love, we are in God's hand.
How strange now, looks the life he makes us lead;
So free we seem, so fettered fast we are!

Robert Browning (1812-89)

I'm dying, dying; thou wilt be content,
For my sad voice will weary thee no more.
Thou'lt hear instead the bells with their lament,
High in the tower sounding all the four.
When past thy door the dead is borne away,
Come out and look, for I am he they bear:
This only, dearest, for God's love I pray,

Come with me to the church, then leave me there.
Come with me to the church, and shed some tears;
Remember I have loved thee many years.

Roadside Song
Translated by Francesca Alexander (1859)

Leopardi introduced the 1830 edition of his 'canti'(which included his recent Pisan poems) with a quotation from Petrarch. His letter of dedication showed his misery at his increasingly failing health.

Accomplished is the end of my brief fable,
Half-way through life, I know my time is spent.

Dear Friends of mine, Let this book be dedicated to you in which I have attempted, as one often does in poetry, to sublimate my grief – a book with which (I cannot say it without tears) I bid farewell to letters and to my studies. I had hoped that these beloved studies would sustain my old age, I believed that with the loss of all other pleasures, all the joys of childhood and of youth, I had yet acquired one treasure which no power, no misfortune could steal away. But I had not yet reached my twentieth year when more than half of that single blessing was snatched away from me by an infirmity of nerves and health which, while it destroyed the value of life for me, yet offered no hope of death; and two years before I was thirty, this work of destruction was completed; and, as I now believe, for ever. You are well aware that I have not even been able to read these pages, and that to correct them, I have had to make use of the eyes and hands of others.

I will complain no more, my dear friends: my consciousness of the extent of my grief is not compatible with lamentation. I have lost everything: I am only a useless block that feels and suffers. Yet now, even now, my friends, I have acquired your friendship and your company; they take the place of my studies, of every hope and delight, and would almost make up for my troubles, if these ailments of mine allowed me to enjoy them as much as I desire, and if I did not know that Fate will soon deprive me of these too, obliging me to wear out the years that may still be left to me, without any civilized comfort, in a place where the dead are happier than the living. But your love will remain with me, and will endure even when my body, which has already ceased to live, has turned to ashes. Farewell. Your Leopardi.

Giacomo Leopardi (1798-1837)
Translated by Iris Origo (1957)

PUCCINI'S DEATH

The Tuscan composer Giacomo Puccini died in 1924.

I remember the last day he spent in Viareggio. It was twilight, and the people were going down to the beach to watch the ceremony of sunset. A breeze stirred the palms along the promenade. The bells of San Paolino, San Andrea, and San Francesco filled the perfumed air: the scent of the flowers, the scent of the pine-groves. The small boats were gliding past the lighthouse far out at sea. The Café Schicchi was bustling with life. Pea, Vianni, Nomellini, Magrini – they were all waiting for the maestro, but Giacomo was in his villa with Toscanini. He was playing *Turandot* on the piano. He looked desperately ill. At the end of the first act he called to Elvira to bring him coffee, then he sipped the black liquid gratefully and went on playing.

'Here Turandot sings,' Giacomo said excitedly, and then turned to Tonio: 'Put a cigarette between my lips.'

Tonio lit a cigarette and put it between his father's lips. Giacomo went on playing. Toscanini was following the score. Giacomo was looking up edgewise to see the expression on the conductor's face. There were tears in Toscanini's eyes. Giacomo winked at me and whispered, 'Eh, boy, do you see that? This music must be good if it makes *testa piccina* (tiny head) cry.'

One by one the lights in the villa went out. The little group, which had gathered together to hear the first reading of *Turandot*, rode through the night to the railway station, moving in darkness like mourners at a funeral. Only Elvira, at the doctor's orders, remained behind. We were going to put Giacomo on the Rome-Paris express. Tonio joined his father in the train. Giacomo lowered a window of the *wagon-lit* and leaned out, saying his farewells to the group standing

228

forlornly on the platform. His last words were to Toscanini: 'Arturo, if anything happens to me, do not abandon my dear beautiful princess, my *Turandot–*'

Then he withdrew hastily: the excitement had brought on a hemorrhage of the throat.

The train began to move away, the wheels turning with a sobbing rhythm. Someone remarked that Verdi had been inspired by the movement of train-wheels to compose the accompaniment of the *"Miserere"* in *Il Trovatore.*

Miserere di un anima gia vicina alla partenza che non ha ritorno.

Pity the soul which is nearing the place whence there is no return.

Dante del Fiorentino (pub. 1952)

Non ho un amico
mi sento solo,
anche la musica
triste mi fa.
Quando la morte,
verrà a trovarmi
sarò felice di riposarmi

I have no friend,
And I feel alone:
Even my music
Fills me with melancholy.
And when death comes
I shall be happy
To take my rest...

Giacomo Puccini (1858-1924)

Beautiful Florence! City of learning, luxury and flowers; serious above all things, seed of myrtle and crown of 'slender laurel'.

Vincigliata. It was there I first saw clouds dissolving in the blue sky, it astonished me greatly, for I had no idea they could melt into the azure in this way, and had always thought they went on getting heavier and heavier until they turned into rain. But no; I watched them disappearing, cloudlet after cloudlet, until nothing was left but the azure. It was a marvellous death – a vanishing in the midst of Heaven.

André Gide (1869-1951) Translated by D. Bussey (1949)

THE ENGLISH CEMETERY

Still, when evening comes in October,
and on the boulevards the fog just lightly veils
the plane trees, as it used to in our day,
between the ivy-covered walls and the cypresses
of the English cemetery, the caretakers
burn twigs and dry laurel.
              The smoke
from the branches is green,
like that of the charcoal makers in the forests
on the mountains.
              Those evenings,
already a bit chilly for us, died with
sweet agony. I loved then to search
for your wrist and to caress it. Then
there were the dim lights, the huge shadows
in the gardens, the gravel, your steps full and calm;
the stone along the walls next to the gates
had, you said, the smell of October and the smoke
smelled of countryside and vineyards.
Your dear mouth opened round in the dark,
soft and submissive grape.
              Now so much time
has passed,
I don't know where you are, perhaps if I
saw you, I wouldn't recognize you. You're certainly
alive and you sometimes think of how much love
there was, during those years, between us, of how much
life has passed by. And sometimes in your reverie,
as in my own, the one who speaks to you now, a vain
and unbearable pain moans to you;
a painful desire to return, such as
perhaps the poor dead have, to live
there one more time, to see again

that which you were, to travel still
through those evenings of a time which no longer exists,
which no longer has any place,
even if I sometimes go down these Florentine
boulevards where the fog just lightly
veils the plane trees, and in the gardens
they burn the melancholy fires of laurel.

Franco Fortini (1917-) Translated by Lawrence Smith (1981)

FUNERE MERSIT ACERBO

*This sonnet was written on the death of Carducci's infant son, Dante. It is
addressed to the poet's brother (also named Dante) who took his own life a few years
earlier.*

O thou who 'neath the flower-clad Tuscan hill
Dost slumber, by whose side our father lies,
Hast thou not heard e'en now a soft voice thrill
The grass upon thy grave with plaintive cries?

It is my little son who at thy chill
Door knocks; he who renews thee in the wise
Great name. The life that thou to bear didst still
So bitter find, O brother, he too flies.

Ah no, 'mid painted flower-beds he played,
Laughed at blithe visions, till the shadow fell
On him, and thrust him downwards to your cold

Lone shore. Receive him thou, for he must dwell
In the dark seats; the sweet sun to behold
He turns, and to his mother cries for aid.

Giosué Carducci (1835-1907) Translated by E. Tribe (1921)

SAVONAROLA

*Fra Girolamo Savonarola came to Florence from Ferrara in 1489 and took a brief
but powerful hold over the city.*

Under the influence of Savonarola there was a brief and bloodthirsty
return to the Middle Ages. It was a tragic end to the most glorious

century in Florentine history. Individual liberty was destroyed for the sake of what Savonarola considered a greater liberty: the secrets of the Confessional and the privacy of family life were violated, and servants were encouraged to turn informers against their masters. Hideous tortures were devised for such offences as gambling, and costume was made the subject of severe legislation. Fasting became the order of the day; the 'Burning of Vanities' replaced the Medicean festivals. Street urchins were organized into moral police, who trotted from house to house to collect 'luxuries' such as ornaments, mirrors, cosmetics, and bric-à-brac, profane writings such as those of Pulci and Boccaccio, and, above all, any representation of pagan deities and of the sinful nude, for the virtuous bonfire. It was the reign of religious mania and militant Puritanism, and again the city was divided as of old. Yet many an historian has been devoted to Savonarola and indulgent to his excesses. The revulsion of the public was ferocious when it came in 1498, 'Prophet! now is the time for a miracle!' shouted the mob, when Savonarola was hanged from the gibbet and a fire kindled beneath him. In contrast with the yoke he had laid upon poor nature, the so-called tyranny of Lorenzo seemed positively Utopian. For as Guicciardini wrote in the 1530's, 'Florence could not have had a better or a more delightful tyrant.'

Harold Acton (1904-)

SAVONAROLA'S DEATH

Savonarola was executed as a heretic in 1498.

From the papal tribune the monks were led to the stand where sat the Eight of Justice. Here Piero Parenti, the Gonfalonier of Justice, read the verdict of the secular court which found Savonarola guilty of having fostered civil strife, been instrumental in driving out the Medici and having connived at the death of the five prominent citizens who were executed for high treason and conspiracy.

At last the ordeal was over. It was three o'clock. The formalities had lasted from eight in the morning. Fra Silvestro Maruffi, who was the first to be hanged, almost ran up the ladder. At the top, as the executioner fastened the iron collar around his neck, he called down to Savonarola: 'Father Girolamo, see how a knight of Jesus Christ dies with joy in his heart...' He wanted to say something more, but the

Fra Bartolommeo (1472-1517), Fra Girolamo Savonarola
Museum of San Marco (Photo Alinari)

executioner pushed him off the ladder and the body swung free. For a few moments Silvestro's pitiful cries resounded through the Piazza: *Jesu, miserere! Christe, miserere!* 'Jesus, have mercy! Christ, have mercy!' Then only did the executioner apply the garrot.

Fra Domenico Buonvicini came next. As he walked to the stake he intoned the psalm: 'In thee O God, I have trusted.' A priest walking by his side cautioned him: 'Do not sing so loud, it is unbecoming!' Halfway up the ladder, Domenico turned to the crowd and called out: 'I assure you that all of Fra Girolamo's prophecies will go into fulfillment...The Church will be purified. The Holy Spirit will send his heavenly fire...' The executioner ordered him to stop talking. When Domenico dropped from the ladder he died instantly. The bodies of the two monks hung at the two extremities of the crossbeam. The place of honour, in the middle, was reserved for the greatest offender, the heresiarch and arch criminal, as the verdict called Fra Girolamo.

While Savonarola walked slowly to the stake, some Compagnacci broke through the police lines and slashed at his bare legs and feet with their knives and daggers. He paid no attention and probably did not even feel the injuries.

A poor old woman came close to him and offered a crust of bread. 'Take and eat, Blessed Father Girolamo!' He smiled broadly at her and said: 'Thank you very much, my dear daughter, but I need no food now. I have so little a way to go. In a moment I will be in the mansions on high having sup with my Lord and Saviour.'

Before ascending the ladder he asked the executioner to be so kind and tie a rope around his shirt 'for modesty's sake.' The executioner harshly refused. Not even the humiliation of appearing naked before the people was to be spared him. At the foot of the ladder he was assailed by the cry: 'If you are able to perform miracles, now is the time to show us!' The executioner tied his hands behind his back and pushed him towards the Compagnacci to give them an opportunity to spit upon him and strike and scratch his face. When he climbed the ladder his face was covered with blood. On the top rung he stood still, turned around and faced the awe-stricken crowd. How often had he not seen the Florentines gather at his feet in the great Duomo? His eyes traveled over that sea of humanity from left to right and back again from right to left. He tugged at the rope around his wrists as if he wanted to free his right hand in order to raise it in blessing as he had always done when facing a congregation. But the executioner struck him a blow from behind which caused him to fall. Savonarola was dead at once. To amuse the Compagnacci the executioner raised the dead man's shirt with a stick and committed other vile indignities on the body.

At precisely 3:30 in the afternoon the huge pile of faggots was set on fire and the smoke rose in a thick column hiding the three suspended bodies from view. When the flames leaped up they burned the rope around Savonarola's wrists. In the same instant a strong breeze blew into the Piazza. The flames were dispersed and the smoke wafted away. The bodies of the three monks which had been hidden by the curtain of smoke and flame, became visible once more.

Whether it was the temporary cessation of the heat or a last spasm of life which shook Savonarola's frame, the fact remains and is attested to by a number of eye-witnesses, that all at once the dead man's right hand with two fingers uplifted in blessing, rose to the height of his shoulders.

'*Miracolo! Miracolo!* A miracle! a miracle!' roared the crowd scattering in all directions. Pandemonium swept the Piazza. A wail as of a thousand damned souls went up. Women screamed and sobbed. The Compagnacci filled the air with curses and execrations. Men, women, monks, and nuns fought their way out of the Piazza. In the stampede many children were trampled. The halberdiers were pushed aside and the horses of the lancers reared in panic. The members of the Signoria and the papal legates, Romolino in the lead, climbed down from their tribunal and scurried for safety into the palace.

Then the wind subsided and a crepitating pillar of black smoke and flames shot upward removing Savonarola forever from the eyes of men...

Thus went to God the boy from Ferrara whose mother predicted that his mission in life would be a terrible one.

Pierre Van Paasen (pub. 1961)

LOVE SONG

'Sor Colonello, mi da il congedo,
    Per andar a ca';
C'è la mia amorosa
    Ch' a letto sta ma'.

'Il congeda ti sia gia' dato,
    Pur che ci va,
Pur che ci va in compagnia
    De' bravi soldà.'

Quando furon dentro il castello,
   Sentiron suonar:
'É la campana della mia amorosa,
   Me la vanno a portar.'

'Fermati, fermati pur un tantino,
   Riposati un po'!'
'Vo' dar un bacio alla mia amorosa,
   E poi me ne vo.

'Parlami, parlami, bocchin d'amore,
   Parlami un po'!'
Tu non vedi che l'è estina,
   Parla non ti può.'

'Addio Padre, addio mia Madre,
   Addio fratei!
Se ci fusse la mia amorosa
   Contento sarei.'

This translation was given to Ruskin in 1859.

'Colonel, give me leave a little,
   That I home may go:
For my love in bed lies fading,
   Sick, and sinking low.'

'Leave to go I give thee,
   Also shall thou have
With thee, for thine honour,
   Brothers of the brave.'

As they reached the village.
   All the bells did ring:
'These are the bells for my true love,
   News of death they bring.'

'Stay, poor soldier, rest a little,
   Weary must you be.'
'I will kiss my love and leave her,
   There's no rest for me.'

'Little mouth, so loving,
   Speak to me, I pray!
Never more those lips can open,
   Life has passed away.'

'Farewell father, mother, brothers,'
   Said he as he went,
'If my love were with me
   I were well content.'

A Roadside Song
Translated by Francesca Alexander (1859)

PARTING

This was their last afternoon together, and, as they left the city by the road that passes through Diecimo and Bettone on its way to Bagni di Lucca, she wished Piers also to recognize the finality of their parting so that, until they parted, they might be at peace: not to mock at her renunciation and refuse to believe in it, but to give it strength by his acceptance of it. Though it was inevitable that they should meet in the company of others when he visited Sparkenbroke, she wished him to promise that he would never seek her out, never write to her, never use his power over her.

The road, lined with silver birch, by which they had been travelling was left behind. A small town, Ponte a Moriano, appeared ahead. Before we enter the town, she thought, I will ask for his pledge, but at the outskirts a little stream shone at the roadside and Piers said:

'Look. I love streams that flow close to a road. Perhaps because I used to play in the stream at the bottom of the churchyard at home.'

He drove on, through the town, past the bridge spanning the Serchio, and she had not said what she intended to say. She lay back, treasuring the instants and thinking that now, whenever she crossed from the Rectory to the church, she would be reminded of the stream at Ponte a Moriano. Is that true? When I'm old and Piers, it may be, is dead, shall I remember, day by day, this stream at Ponte a Moriano? Is this the past? and she looked around desperately to seize it, to catch sight of the stream once again, but it was gone. I shall never forget those flaming things hung out on the walls. 'What are they – those red-gold pillars?' He said they were maize, set out to dry.

The town died away into a straggle of white cottages and soon they were in open country again, the broad Serchio on their left and, on their right, pine-clad hills, a heavy green, cut by blocks of gold. The river bent sharply, and on either hand were steep mountains that carried the eye upwards to a still, empty sky; the Serchio vanished, a great avenue of planes shut out the sky until suddenly the valley opened on a mass of silver birch. Soon the square tower of Diecimo stood up to their left and ahead of them was another village, Bettone, which seemed asleep and the more asleep because in one of its higher windows was a piece of red material, perhaps a petticoat, which hung, limp and dead, on the sunlit wall as though it had been forgotten.

Charles Morgan (1894-1958)

SHELLEY'S DEATH

In 1822 Shelley was drowned while returning to Lerici after meeting Leigh Hunt in Livorno. His friend, Edward Trelawney, was in Livorno at the time.

On Monday, the 8th of July, 1822, I went with Shelley to his bankers, and then to a store. It was past one p.m. when we went on board our respective boats, – Shelley and Williams to return to their home in the Gulf of Spezzia; I in the *Bolivar* to accompany them into the offing. When we were under weigh, the guard-boat boarded us to overhaul our papers. I had not got my port clearance, the captain of the port having refused to give it to the mate. I had often gone out without. The officer of the Health Office consequently threatened me with fourteen days' quarantine. It was hopeless to think of detaining my friends. Williams had been for days fretting and fuming to be off; they had no time to spare, it was past two o'clock, and there was very little wind.

Sullenly and reluctantly I re-anchored, furled my sails, and with a ship's glass watched the progress of my friends' boat. My Genoese mate observed, – 'They should have sailed this morning at three or four a.m., instead of three p.m. They are standing too much in shore; the current will set them there.'

I said, 'They will soon have the land-breeze.'

'Maybe,' continued the mate, 'she will soon have too much breeze; that gaff topsail is foolish in a boat with no deck and no sailor on board.' Then pointing to the S.W., 'Look at those black lines and the

238

dirty rags hanging on them out of the sky – they are a warning; look at the smoke on the water; the devil is brewing mischief.'

There was a sea-fog, in which Shelley's boat was soon after enveloped, and we saw nothing more of her.

...I did not leave the *Bolivar* until dark. During the night it was gusty and showery, and the lightning flashed along the coast: at daylight I returned on board and resumed my examinations of the crews of the various boats which had returned to the port during the night. They either knew nothing, or would say nothing. My Genoese, with the quick eye of a sailor, pointed out on board a fishing-boat, an English-made oar that he thought he had seen in Shelley's boat, but the entire crew swore by all the saints in the calendar that this was not so. Another day was passed in horrid suspense. On the morning of the third day I rode to Pisa. Byron had returned to the Lanfranchi Palace. I hoped to find a letter from the Villa Magni: there was none. I told my fears to Hunt and then went upstairs to Byron. When I told him, his lip quivered, and his voice faltered as he questioned me. I sent a courier to Leghorn to despatch the *Bolivar* to cruise along the coast whilst I mounted my horse and rode in the same direction. I also despatched a courier along the coast, to go as far as Nice. On my arrival at Via Reggio I heard that a punt, a water-keg, and some bottles had been found on the beach. These things I recognized as having been in Shelley's boat when he left Leghorn. Nothing more was found for seven or eight days, during which time of painful suspense I patrolled the coast with the coast-guard, stimulating them to keep a good look-out by the promise of a reward.

It was not until many days after this that my worst fears were confirmed. Two bodies were found on the shore – one near Via Reggio, which I went and examined. The face and hands, and parts of the body not protected by the dress, were fleshless. The tall, slight figure, the jacket, the volume of Aeschylus in one pocket, and Keats's poems in the other, doubled back, as if the reader, in the act of reading, had hastily thrust it away, were all too familiar to me to leave a doubt on my mind that this mutilated corpse was any other than Shelley's. The other body was washed on shore three miles distant from Shelley's, near the tower of Migliarino, at the Bocca Lericcio. I went there at once.

...It was not until three weeks after the wreck of the boat that a third body was found – four miles from the other two.

Three white wands had been stuck in the sand to mark the Poet's grave, but as they were at some distance from each other, we had to cut a trench thirty yards in length, in the line of the sticks, to ascertain the exact spot, and it was nearly an hour before we came upon the grave.

...Even Byron was silent and thoughtful. We were startled and drawn together by a dull hollow sound that followed the blow of a mattock; the iron had struck a skull, and the body was soon uncovered. Lime had been strewn on it; this, or decomposition, had the effect of staining it of a dark and ghastly indigo colour. Byron asked me to preserve the skull for him; but remembering that he had formerly used one as a drinking-cup, I was determined Shelley's should not be so profaned. The limbs did not separate from the trunk, as in the case of Williams's body, so that the corpse was removed entire into the furnace. I had taken the precaution of having more and larger pieces of timber, in consequence of my experience of the day before of the difficulty of consuming a corpse in the open air with our apparatus. After the fire was well kindled we repeated the ceremony of the previous day; and more wine was poured over Shelley's dead body than he had consumed during his life. This with the oil and salt made the yellow flames glisten and quiver. The heat from the sun and fire was so intense that the atmosphere was tremulous and wavy. The corpse fell open and the heart was laid bare. The frontal bone of the skull, where it had been struck with the mattock, fell off; and, as the back of the head rested on the red-hot bottom bars of the furnace, the brains literally seethed, bubbled, and boiled as in a cauldron, for a very long time.

Byron could not face this scene, he withdrew to the beach and swam off to the *Bolivar*. Leigh Hunt remained in the carriage. The fire was so fierce as to produce a white heat on the iron, and to reduce its contents to grey ashes. The only portions that were not consumed were some fragments of bones, the jaw and the skull, but what surprised us all was that the heart remained entire. In snatching this relic from the fiery furnace, my hand was severely burnt; and had any one seen me do the act I should have been put into quarantine.

Edward Trelawney (1792-1881)

Fiesole

I walked back from Fiesole on an unforgettable summer's evening: I looked down over the olive trees to the Valley of the Arno, where the

240

domes and towers of Florence could be seen illuminated by the last half-hour of sunlight. The sky was already pink at the edges, offering that delicious Italian assurance that the sun would shine tomorrow. The cicadas were trilling in the fields and gardens, and the stone walls held the heat of the day. As I picked out Brunelleschi's dome and Giotto's tower, I heard a stealthy clatter near at hand, and, glancing over a stone wall, saw on a lower level two white oxen, with horns like harp frames, come slowly under the olives behind a plough. The farmer, like an Irishman, was stealing a scratch crop. I called down and asked what he intended to grow. He looked up, and I found myself gazing at the lean taut face of Cosimo de Medici.

'Melons', he replied.

I had been to visit two English friends, rich and elderly, who were trying to find peace in a troubled world. They had tried South Africa, where they had doubled their capital in a gold-mine merger, but it was too far from Europe. Perhaps Italy was the answer. I was anxious to see them, for, of course, there is no answer to their problem! Peace, if it exists, exists only in one's self.

They had rented a villa below Fiesole, quite in the old style. There was nothing the English colony of a century ago would not have recognized: the brown-washed building with its central tower, standing in its *podere* of farmland: the box-edged garden with its fountain and the double line of lemon trees in terracotta tubs; the tiled shelter in which the lemons are placed under sacking in winter. It was all there, even to the Italian family: the butler-handyman in white linen coat and black trousers, ready to receive guests; the cook, his ample, sallow wife; a dark-eyed daughter busy about some household task. It looked the same on the surface, but, of course, it was all different. The wages alone would have ruined the Brownings in a month. Rent was high, living was expensive, but, above all, it was lonely. There is now no English colony in the old sense. Today the villas of Tuscany are prestige homes for wealthy manufacturers from Turin and Milan.

'I think,' said my friend, 'when our lease is up next spring, we shall probably try Monte Carlo.'

I said good-bye, feeling that the Anglo-Florentine sunset has definitely set over Fiesole. But one well-known English pen continues to write on those hills, In the beautiful *La Pietra,* which dates from 1460, Harold Acton has written his distinguished books on the Medici and the Bourbons of Naples. The Italian garden which his father created so skilfully, a wonderful composition of box hedges, terraces, fountains, statues, and even a greenwood theatre, deserves to be remembered as an English contribution to the Florentine scene.

I walked on to the main road through steep and narrow lanes confined by stone walls. The sloping hillside was dotted with villa after villa, each one escorted by guardian cypress trees: a landscape unchanged in appearance since the nineteenth century.

H.V. Morton (1892-1979)

Michelangelo

Michelangelo passed most of his old age in Rome. His letters show that he missed Florence, although he refused to return, and found his increasing infirmity hard to bear as it intruded more and more into his work.

About St. Peter's Dome. August 17 1557

...this error accrued because I was unable to go there often enough on account of my old age. And whereas I thought said vault would be finished by now, it will not be finished during the whole winter. If one could die of shame or grief, I would not be alive.

Michelangelo (1475-1564)
Translated by C. Speroni (1963)

From The Old Age of Michelangelo

Sometimes the light falls here too as at Florence
Circled by low hard hills, or in the quarry
Under its half-hewn cliffs, where that collection
Of pale rough blocks, still lying at all angles on the
    dust-white floor
Waits, like a town of tombs.
    I finish nothing I begin.
And the dream sleeps in the stone, to be unveiled
Or half-unveiled, the lurking nakedness;
Luminous as a grapeskin, the cold marble mass
Of melted skeins, chains, veils and veins,
Bosses and hollows, muscular convexities,

242

Supple heroic surfaces, tense drums
And living knots and cords of love:
– Sleeps in the stone, and is unveiled
Or half-unveiled, the body's self a veil,
By the adze and the chisel, and the mind
Impelled by torment.
    In the empty quarry
The light waits, and the tombs wait,
For the coming of a dream.

F. Templeton Prince (1912-)

JANUARY 1559

I have nothing else to tell you. I am all yours, old, blind, and deaf, and
in poor agreement with my hands and my person.

Michelangelo (1475-1564)
Translated by C. Speroni (1963)

LXV

TO GIORGIO VASARI

ON THE BRINK OF DEATH

Giunto è già

Now hath my life across a stormy sea
    Like a frail bark reached that wide port where all
    Are bidden, ere the final reckoning fall
    Of good and evil for eternity.
Now know I well how that fond phantasy
    Which made my soul the worshipper and thrall
    Of earthly art, is vain; how criminal
    Is that which all men seek unwillingly.
Those amorous thoughts which were so lightly dressed,
    What are they when the double death is nigh?
    The one I know for sure, the other dread.

Painting nor sculpture now can lull to rest
  My soul that turns to His great love on high,
  Whose arms to clasp us on the cross were spread.

Michelangelo Buonarroti (1475-1564)
Translated by J. Addington Symonds (1840-93)

Michelangelo (1475-1564), Head of an Old Man Collezione Mannelli (Photo Alinari)

B.C.

1000	The Iron Age
900	Villanovian peasants and fishermen settle on the banks of the Arno
700- 500	Etruscan civilization at its height
480- 290	Expansion of Roman power
474	Etruscans defeated by the Greeks in a sea battle at Cumae
218- 203	Hannibal in Italy
264- 201	Punic Wars
70- 19	Virgil (Publius Vergilius Maro)

A.D.

250	Martyrdom of San Miniato
167- 600	Invasions by Goths, Lombards, Franks, Byzantines etc.
476	Downfall of Rome in the West
1115	Death of Countess Matilda of Tuscany
1000-1300	Main period of struggle between the Guelphs and Ghibellines
1240-1302	Cimabue (Cenni di Pepi)
1265-1321	Dante Alighieri
1267-1337	Giotto di Bondone
1296	Arnolfo di Cambio starts the cathedral in Florence
1299-1301	The building of the Palazzo Vecchio in Florence
1302-1310	The pulpit at Pisa Cathedral by Giovanni Pisano
1304-1374	Francesco Petrarch
1311	Duccio's Maestà
1314-1321	Dante's Divine Comedy
1347-1351	The Black Death strikes Europe
1348-1353	Boccaccio's Decameron
1377-1446	Filippo Brunelleschi
1378-1455	Lorenzo Ghiberti
1378	Ciompi Revolt in Florence
1386-1466	Donatello (Donato de Nicolo di Betto Bardi)
1406	Florence conquers Pisa
1401-1428	Masaccio (Tomasso (Guido di Pietro) di Giovanni di Guidi)
1406	Florence conquers Pisa
1387-1455	Fra Angelico
1397-1475	Paolo Uccello
1409	Council of Pisa
1420-1492	Piero della Francesca
1420-1436	Brunelleschi's dome

1423-1433	Florence and Venice at war with Milan
1434-1465	Cosimo de Medici rules Florence
1434-1441	Florence and Venice fight the Visconti
1405-1464	Pope Pius II
1448-1494	Domenico Ghirlandaio
1452-1519	Leonardo da Vinci
1469-1492	Lorenzo de Medici rules Florence
1471-1484	Pope Sixtus IV
1475-1564	Michelangelo Buonarroti
1478	The Pazzi Conspiracy
1478-1480	Florence, Venice and Milan at war with the Pope and Naples and Siena
1483-1520	Raphael Santi
1494	The Medici expelled from Florence
1498	Girolamo Savonarola burnt as a heretic
1498-1512	Machiavelli second Chancellor of Florence
1512	The Medici return to power in Florence
1527-1530	Florence – a republic
1530-1537	Alessandro de Medici rules Florence
1537-1574	Cosimo de Medici in power
1555	Siena finally falls to Florence
1561	Academy of drawing founded in Florence
1564-1642	Galilei Galileo
1737	Death of Gian Gastone, the last of the Medici Tuscany goes to Francis of Lorraine
1749-1803	Vittorio Alfieri – poet
1796	Napoleon's first Italian campaign
1798-1837	Giacomo Leopardi
1835-1907	Giosuè Carducci
1848-1849	First war of independence
1849	Republic of Rome
1858-1924	Giacomo Puccini
1859	Second war of independence Battle of Solferino Expulsion of Grand Duke Leopold
1860	Cavour comes to an agreement with Napoleon III and Tuscany joins Piedmont
1861	Victor Emanuel II – King of Italy
1865	Capital moves briefly to Florence
1866	Third war of independence
1870	Rome becomes capital of Italy
1878-1900	Umberto I – King of Italy
1900	Umberto assassinated Victor Emanuel III becomes King
1915	Italy joins the Allies in World War I

1922	Fascists march on Rome
	Mussolini takes over
1940	Italy enters World War II on the side of the Nazis
1943	Anti-fascist strikes
	Mussolini arrested then freed
	Badoglio's government joins the Allies
1944	Allies reach Florence
1945	Growth of resistance movement. Liberation of Florence. German surrender
1946	Victor Emanuel III abdicates. His son Umberto II is exiled following referendum
	Italy is established as a republic
1966	Great Flood in Florence

254

Harold Acton, *Florence:* J. Addington Symonds, *The Renaissance in Italy*; *The Sonnets of Michelangelo* and *Tomasso Campanella*; C. M. Ady, *Lorenzo de Medici* and *Renaissance Italy*; A. Akhmatova, *Poems*; V. Alfieri, *Memoirs*; M. Ayrton, *Golden Sections*; H. Belloc, *Complete Verse*; B. Berenson, *Rumours and Reflections*; *Sunset and Twilight*; E. Barrett Browning, *Complete Verse*; A. Blok *The Twelve and other poems*; A. Boyars *The New Poetry*; G. Butler and F. Templeton Prince from *The Penguin Book of South African Verse*; G. Boccaccio, *The Decameron*; R. Browning, *Complete Works*; Lord Byron, *Complete Works*; I Calvino, *Italian Folk Tales*; H. B. Campbell and E. Punzacch, *A Journey to Florence in 1817*; G. Carducci from *Italian Lyricists of Today*; B. Castiglione, *The Courtier*; B. Cellini, *Memoirs*; K. Clark, *Piero della Francesca*; G. D'Annunzio from *D'Annunzio* by *Phillipe Julien*; Dante, *The Divine Comedy*; C. Day Lewis, *Virgil's Georgics*; *An Italian Visit*; A. Del Conte, *A Portrait of Pasta*; D. Del Fiorentino, *Immortal Bohemian: an intimate memoir of the life of G. Puccini*; N. Douglas, *Alone*; J. Elroy Flecker, *The Collected Poems*; N. Fersin, *The Florentine Fior di Virtù*; R. Flower, *Chianti*; E. M. Forster, *A Room with a View*; *Where Angels Fear to Tread*; F. Fortini from *The New Italian Poetry*; G. Galileo from *The Private Life of Gall* by *Sister Maria Celeste*; A. Gide, *The Fruits of the Earth*; G. Grigson, *Collected Poems 1924-62*; F. Guicciardini, *Counsels and Reflections*; T. Hardy, *Selected Poems*; A. J. C. Hare, *Florence*; N. Hawthorne, *The French and Italian Notebooks*; M. Hazan, *The Classic Italian Cookbook*; S. Heaney, *Fieldwork*; H. Heine, *Pictures of Travel*; E. Hutton, *In Unknown Tuscany*; *Florence and Northern Tuscany*; *Italian Hours*; A. Huxley, *Letters*; E. Jennings, *The Sonnets of Michelangelo*; *Collected Poems*; D. H. Lawrence, *Etruscan Places*; *Collected Poems*; L. Lee, *I Can't Stay Long*; Leigh Hunt, *Autobiography*; Livy, *History of Rome Vol. III*; R. Lowell, *History*; A. Lyall, *The Companion Guide to Tuscany*; N. Machiavelli, *The Prince*; *The Literary Works of;* Y. Maguire, *The Private Life of Lorenzo The Magnificent*; H. Mann, *Horace Walpole Correspondence*; Mary McCarthy, *The Stones of Florence*; C. Morgan, *Sparkenbroke*; H. V. Morton, *A Traveller in Italy*; A. Moorehead, *A Late Education*; F. Moryson, *Journal*; R. C. Namantius, *De Redito Suo*; S. O'Faolain, *Summer in Italy*; U. Ojetti, *As They Seemed to Me*; Iris Origo, *The Merchant of Prato*; *Images and Shadows*; *War in the Vald 'Orcia*; Origo and Heath-Stubbs, *Leopardi: Selected Prose and Poetry*; F. Petrarch, *Sonnets*; W. Pezzini, *The Tuscan Cookbook*; Pius II, *Memoirs of a Renaissance Pope*; Pliny (the Younger), *Letters*; *Collected Shorter Poems*; E. Pound, *Cantos*; V. Pratolini, *The Girls of San Frediano*; S. Rogers, *Italy and other Poems*; A. Ross, *Poems*; J. Ross, *Italian Sketches*; D. G. Rossetti, *Complete Poems*; J. Ruskin, *Mornings in Florence*; *The Works of J. Ruskin*; M. Salvadori, *The*

Labour and the Wounds; P. Bysshe Shelley, *Complete Verse*; O. Sitwell, *On the Continent*; S. Sitwell, *Complete Poems*; T. Smollett, *Travels through France and Italy*; Stendhal, *Rome, Naples and Florence*; D. Thomas, *Selected Letters of*; A. Thorne, *The Sky is Italian*; C. Tomlinson, *Written on Water*; *Penguin Modern Poets*; E. J. Trelawney, *The Last Days of Shelley and Byron*; *Records of Shelley and Byron*; M. Twain, *Innocents Abroad*; G. Vasari, *The Lives of The Artists*; P. van Paasen, *A Crown of Fire*; G. Villani, *Croniche Florentine*; P. Villari, *History*; E. Whipple, *A Famous Corner of Tuscany*; V. Woolf, *Flush*; *A Writer's Diary*.

I would very much like to thank all the people who contributed or advised me in the compiling of this book, paticularly Christopher Burness – my publisher.

My thanks are also due to the following for permission to publish certain copyright material in this anthology.

Cecilia M. Ady and Hodder and Stoughton Ltd. for an extract from *Lorenzo dei Medici and Renaissance Italy.*

An extract from *Vittorio Alfieri: Memoirs* translated by E. R. P. Vincent (1961). Reprinted by permission of Oxford University Press.

Michael Ayrton and Secker & Warburg Ltd. for La Madonna del Parto from *Rudiments of Paradise.*

George Bell 1907 for *Rutilius Claudius Namantius,* trans. George Savage Armstrong.

Hilaire Belloc, Gerald Duckworth & Co Ltd. and A. D. Peters & Co Ltd. for I went to sleep at dawn in Tuscany from *Complete Verse.*

Bernard Berenson, Erich Linder for extracts from *Sunset and Twilight.*

Bernard Berenson, Constable & Co Ltd. and Simon & Schuster Inc. for extracts from *Rumour and Reflection.*

Extracts from *The Twelve and Other Poems* by Alexander Blok, translated by Jon Stallworthy and Peter France (1974) by permission of Methuen London.

Arthur Boyars for Florence: Garibaldi Day 1949 from *New Poetry* by Arthur Boyars.

George Bull (trans) Machiavelli: *The Prince* pp 87, 95 *Penguin Classics,* Revised ed. 1975. Reprinted by permission of Penguin Books Ltd. Copyright © George Bull, 1961, 1975.

George Bull (trans) *Vasari: Lives of the Artists* pp 206, 207, 216, 217-8, 144, 97-8 *Penguin Classics,* Revised ed. 1971. Reprinted by permission of Penguin Books Ltd. Copyright © George Bull, 1965.

J. B. Bury for a paragraph from his *Obituary of Count Rucellai (The Times* 29.4.83).

Prof. Guy Butler for his poem *Giotto's Campanile.*

Italo Calvino for The Florentine from *Italian Folktales,* trans. George Martin (Penguin Books 1982) pp 277-280. Copyright © Giulio Einaudi Editore, s.p.a. 1956. This translation copyright © Harcourt Brace

Jovanovich, Inc. 1980 Reprinted by permission of Penguin Books ltd.

Kenneth Clark and Phaidon Press Ltd. for The Resurrection from *Piero della Francesco* pp 57.

Purgatorio VI and Inferno V & XIII from *The Divine Comedy* by Dante, translated by C. H. Sisson, Carcanet Press 1980, Regnery Gateway Inc.

Dante del Fiorentino and Prentice-Hall Inc. for three excerpts from *Immortal Bohemian* (an intimate memoir of G. Puccini).

Peter Owen (London) Ltd. for an extract from *F. Dostoevsky Letters* translated by E. C. Mayne.

Society of Authors for an excerpt from *Alone* by Norman Douglas.

Raymond Flower and Croom Helm Ltd. for The World (3 pages) from *Chianti*.

E. M. Forster, Edward Arnold Ltd. and Alfred A. Knopf Inc. for extracts from *Where Angels Fear to Tread* and *A Room with a View.*

Franco Fortini, Lawrence Smith (trans) and the University of California Press for The English Cemetery from *The New Italian Poetry*.

André Gide, Secker & Warburg Ltd. and Editions Gallimard for extracts from *Fruits of the Earth.*

F. A. Gragg (trans), George Allen & Unwin and The Putman Publishing Group for an extract from *Memoirs of a Renaissance Pope.*

Geoffrey Grigson for his poem Return to Florence from *Collected Poems 1963-1980.*

Marcella Hazan for extracts from *The Classic Italian Cookbook* by permission of Macmillan, London and Basingstoke and A. M. Heath & Co Ltd.

An excerpt from Ugolino from *Fieldwork* by Seamus Heaney reprinted by permission of Faber and Faber Ltd. and Farrar, Straus and Giroux, Inc. Copyright © 1976, 1979 by Seamus Heaney.

Extracts from *In Unknown Tuscany* and *Florence and Northern Tuscany* by Edward Hutton by permission of Methuen London.

Mrs. Laura Huxley, Chatto & Windus Ltd. and Harper & Row Publishers Inc. for an extract from *Letters of Aldous Huxley*: Ed. Grover Smith.

Elizabeth Jennings and Andre Deutsch for Florence: Design for a City from *A Way of Looking*: Elizabeth Jennings and Macmillan for extracts from *Collected Poems*; Elizabeth Jennings for translations from *The Sonnets of Michelangelo* published by The Folio Society for its members in 1961.

Brace Jovanovich Inc. for extracts from *A Writers Diary* and *Flush.*